MONSTERS OF THE WORLD

Reference Guide

GEORGE LUNSFORD

BEYOND THE FRAY

Publishing

ISBN 13: 978-1-954528-69-7

Cover design: Dauntless Cover Design

Beyond The Fray Publishing, a division of Beyond The Fray, LLC, San Diego, CA
www.beyondthefraypublishing.com

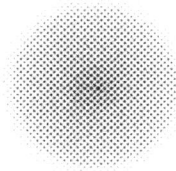

BEYOND THE FRAY

Publishing

CONTENTS

This book is dedicated to the world of people who believe in the things that go bump in the night. I want to thank my amazing wife, who makes all my books readable and shows unconditional support. I also want to thank the incredible people who've allowed me to share their encounters. I also want to apologize to anyone who sent me an encounter that is not in the book. My computer crashed, and I almost lost everything, including the book.

Here are the people who have encounters in the book:
Jonny Elliott, Andy Booth, Mark Farnell, Ron Coxy Cox, Paul Glover, Michelle & Brandon Poye, Steven Glenn, Ricky Crumbly, Maria Portillo, William Roock, Danny Barnwell, Kelly Petrosky, Susan Savatovic, James Hutchinson, David Parker, Glen Bourassa, Anthony Shields, James Bobo Fey, Jami Peters, Kevin L. Peterson Jr., Don S. Kindred, Curt Brueggeman, Timothy J. O'Brien, Ozzy Mason, Cahni Konig, Rosanna Brookhouser, Justin English.

INTRODUCTION

Monsters of The World is about creatures that may or may not exist. I personally believe that these creatures exist. Many modern scientists only believe what the governments allow them to believe. These creatures are considered to be cryptids.

For those of you who may not know, cryptids are animals the cryptozoologists believe may exist somewhere in the wild but are not believed to exist by mainstream science. There are around 18,000 new species found each year. Most of them are small like bugs, plants, or reptiles; however, not all are small; an elephant species and a new species of orangutan were found just a few years ago. Science does not always keep up with reality. There has been tons of proof about some of these creatures, but with nobody on the examination table, it makes most but not all scientists disagree without proof of existence.

Don't get me wrong, some scientists have come around to believe that these creatures may exist. The early people in lands all around the world talk about some of these creatures. They told about them and passed down the stories about them. Yet many modern people only believe what scientists tell them is real. I, on the other hand, believe that the world hides many things from us and will only allow us to see what we can handle.

So step outside of the world you know, and open your mind to the possibility of what could be. I will give you information about each creature, including the origin, description, sightings, and in some cases personal encounters from the people who lived them. This book will introduce you to fifteen creatures from each of the seven continents.

This book is a small cross section of creatures that may or may not exist. I looked through hundreds of pages about different cryptid creatures around the world and chose these for your enjoyment.

Part One

ASIA

We are starting in Asia, which includes forty-eight countries, including Japan, China, and India, to name a few. Let's start with a classic Asian creature, the dragon.

ASIAN DRAGON

The dragon is the most iconic symbol of Asia. There is no consensus on the origin of the Chinese dragon. The earliest known depiction of a dragon is a stylist C-shaped representation carved in jade. Found in eastern Inner Mongolia, it belonged to the Hongshan culture, which thrived between 4500 and 3000 BCE. The

Chinese dragon appears to be a composition of different animals. The body of a snake, scales of a carp, antlers of a stag, face of a camel, talons of eagles, ears of a bull, feet of a tiger, and the eyes of a lobster. Sometimes it has a flaming pearl under its chin. Occasionally they have batlike wings. They have four legs like a lion and can run on land or fly in the air. The dragons have acquired an almost unlimited range of supernatural powers. It is said to be able to disguise itself as a silkworm or become as large as the universe. It can fly among the clouds, hide in or turn into water or even fire, can become invisible, or glow in the dark.

One of the earliest recorded sightings of dragons was Marco Polo. He traveled the world, recording his trip and the things he saw and encountered. Marco Polo told about an encounter with the Great Serpent of Karazhan. It was enormous snake that was twenty-five feet long, with a ten-foot-wide wingspan, seven and a half feet thick, with two short legs near the head, two large powerful legs near the base of the tail, three claws on each leg, large eyes, and jaws wide enough to swallow a man. It approached them without any fear of man, then let out a roar and in a single motion flew off in the sky. The story was written about in the book called *The Travels of Marco Polo*, written by Marco Polo and Rustichello da Pisa, in 1300, and has been adapted into the game of *World of Warcraft*.

The last official sighting of a dragon in China was reported 11 May 1889.

At Sie-fu village about 30 li (9.32 miles) from Nanch'ang, the capital of Kiangsi, a white dragon was seen on the twelfth of April. Dragons like water, and it had rained since about the middle of March straight on, ending on that day in a most tremendous hailstorm, which smashed in the roofs of many of the country people's huts. Suddenly a powerful fishy smell became perceptible, and people coming in from the fields reported the presence of a huge creature, extending about two mows, (about a third of an acre) disporting itself by wriggling and squirming in a pool of water. The next day a few people ventured out to see it; it was white, with scales about two feet in size, with a horned head, claws, and a long tail. On March 18, fine weather returned, and the dragon was gone.

While there are tons of sightings, none are considered official. There are tons of videos on YouTube that I saw. Some people claim they are all hoaxes, but others looked real. I can usually tell if they are CGI, but some appeared to be real. There is a video of a dead dragon found on the coast of a village in China. Chinese officials came and took possession of the creature's body, never to be seen again. Some locals near the mountain range near the border of China and Laos have videoed dragons flying with a camera phone. I don't know if you believe, but I am a believer.

MONGOLIAN DEATH WORM

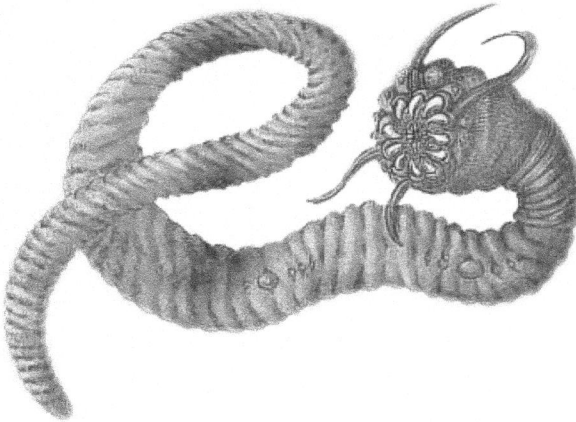

The Mongolian death worm has been stalking the sands of the Gobi Desert for many years. This creature moves beneath the sand and creates waves in the sand as it moves along. The Mongolian death worm is also called Olgoi-Khorkhoi or Allghoi Khorkhoi, which is translated as intestinal worm. Given the name by the native Mongolians because of its blood-red color, it is the approximate length of human intestines, anywhere from two to seven feet long. They say the front of the worm is all mouth of teeth. The worm is known to spew a corrosive yellow saliva and generate an electric discharge. It's said that even just touching the worm can kill you. They are able to sense vibration on the sand and are able to move very fast under the sand. They can reach enough speed to shoot out of the sand to attack their prey. They can attack and take down things as big as a human to a camel. If the death worm preys on an animal, they leave eggs inside the corpse of the animal. When the eggs hatch, they have food to eat. Some scientists believe that the death worm isn't a worm at all but is a venomous snake or even a legless burrowing lizard. The Mongolian death worm's skin is an exoskeleton, which molts whenever it gets injured. The worms are said to only wander the sands in June and July. Supposedly when it rains, they move to the surface.

The first reported sighting of the death worm was in 1927 when American paleontologist Roy Chapman Andrews first saw the tail of the worm. The locals described it as the Allghoi Khorkhoi.

In the 1930s, an expedition went into the Gobi Desert, looking to find the worm. They sighted a red creature that resembled the intestines of a human. The creature disappeared into the sand and escaped.

Another expedition was conducted between 1946 and 1949, and they went deep inside the desert to find proof of the existence of the Mongolian death worm, hoping to compare any of their sightings to ones from the locals.

There is a famous story among the nomads that a young boy was followed by a worm, and near his home, his dead body was found. It was believed that he died as result of touching the worm. The family saw a trail in the sand. The family wanted to get revenge on the animal that did it, but they followed the trail out to the desert and were never seen again.

On one expedition by Freeman, their local interpreter told them about an incident that had happened to another team of expeditioners that traveled to Suji's home village. One of them was poking the sand with an iron rod, and then something felt wrong. Upon reaching him, he was found dead. Others felt a sudden shake in the ground and then saw something round coming out of the sand. It scared them, and they ran for their lives.

In 2005 an entire village had been shifted in the sand after they reported sightings of the Mongolian death worm. It was believed that the worms used their tunneling ability to move the village off its base. Was this a prerequisite for attacks or a warning to the village?

I don't know if the death worms are real, but the Mongolian nomads have told stories of them for a long time.

HIBAGON

A statue of Hibagon and a signboard featuring a Hibagon character at a
visitor center in Shobara, Hiroshima Prefecture

Asia has offered up a dragon and a death worm; now from Japan
we get a version of Bigfoot.

Bigfoot can be and is in every part of the world, or at least a version
of Bigfoot. This is not what you might call a normal Bigfoot. The
legend of the Hibagon is different. Ok, let's jump in.

Most people think that Japan is small, but it is the seventeenth biggest country in Asia and the sixty-fourth biggest in the world. It has around 94% of the land area of California. People also think with a population of 125.8 million people, there is no such thing as monsters there. But wait, 73% of Japan is forest and mountains. You may be thinking, ok, there is room for Hibagon to roam without having to encounter people, but is there enough food to the sustain a group of Hibagon. Well, there are plenty of animals for them to eat.

Hibagon is described as reddish brown or black, sometimes having a patch of white fur on its chest or arms. It has a foul smell like almost all Bigfoot-type creatures. The things that make this creature stand out are the fierce face covered with bristles, a snub nose, and its intense intelligent eyes. Hibagon has an unusually large head in the shape of an inverted triangle. These creatures are closer to the size of the yeti. They are around 1.5 meters to 1.7 meters, or around 5 feet tall. They weigh around 80 to 90 kilograms, or around 180 lbs. The name of this creature comes from the local animal control board. There are some theories of what this creature could be, and it ranges from a gorilla, a wild man, or a deserter from the Japanese chefs, and even a person ravaged by radiation from the attack on Hiroshima.

The main area of the sightings was around Mount Hiba, which is a mountain in Hiroshima Prefecture, between 1970 and 1982.

The first sighting of Hibagon occurred in early 1970 when a group of elementary school kids were picking wild mushrooms in the forest of Mount Hiba, when they came up on an apelike creature. It came crashing noisily through the brush. The creature was agitated by the presence of the kids, and the creature angrily started snapping branches. It made excessive noises to intimidate the kids to leave. The kids were scared to death, and they ran back to tell their teachers what had happened. A group adults gathered together to investigate what the kids had seen. They returned to the area where the kids had seen the creature and found that the creature had left but had smashed down underbrush and broken and twisted branches thicker than a kid could have broken.

The next sighting in 1970 was when it was spotted by a truck driver. The driver said he saw a gorilla-like creature, standing upright like a man, walk across a field near a dam, then run across the road, disappearing into the forest. The truck driver described it as being bipedal but hunched over with extremely long arms dragging along the ground and a snouted face.

Just a few days later on July 23, 1970, the creature came walking out of tall grass, surprising a farmer. The farmer described it as being as tall as an average man, covered with black fur, and it had a terrible face, but the eyes had intelligence. It was also seen walking through a rice field in the town of Sijo.

In December 1970, some very strange tracks in the snow measuring twenty-one centimeters in length were found near Mount Hiba. In the following years, more tracks were found, with one of the longest track sets that went on for three hundred meters, and also one of the largest tracks, of thirty centimeters.

One of the most significant sightings was on August 15, 1974, when a motorist spotted a large black creature walking on four legs on the side of the road. The motorist believed it was a bear until the creature noticed the car and stood up on two legs and walked off. The motorist stopped and jumped out with a camera and took a picture of the creature. You can find it online; it is not good quality and looks like it was shot with a 110 point-and-shoot camera.

KAPPA

Let's take a look at another Japanese creature called the Kappa. This creature inhabits ponds and rivers. One nickname is "water child," and it gets that nickname because it is up to five feet tall. The Kappa has webbed hands and feet. It's at home in the water and clumsier on land. Their skin is scaly like a reptile with skin color that varies. Their skin can be yellow, green, and even blue. The Kappa is a humanoid figure with a tortoise shell on its back. They are said to have long hair shaped like a bowl-cut haircut. Their mouth resembles a snapping turtle beak. All Kappa have a small bowl-like dent on the top of their head that holds a small pool of water called the "sara." This water is thought to be the source of the Kappa's magical powers. They must keep their sara full whenever they venture onto land or forfeit their strength, magical powers, and even their life. It is said that if you find a Kappa with little or no sara and you refill it, the Kappa will be eternally grateful. It will help you with whatever you require for the rest of your life.

The Kappa will cause mischief in the form of harmless jokes like making fart sounds and looking up a woman's kimono. However, they also can be very dangerous. The Kappa have been known to drown livestock, eat and kidnap children, and force themselves on women. They drink the blood of their victims, whether it be livestock or children; and they very much enjoy sexually assaulting women. Kappa are generally considered to be feared, but there are some instances when the Kappa are considered to be generous. The Kappa are said to have given humans the knowledge of bone setting and the use of medical salves.

According to folklore, Kappa are obsessed with an object called Shirikodama—which is a mysterious jewel thought to contain a person's lifeforce that is located in the shiri, otherwise known as the anus. The belief is that most of the attacks from the Kappa are made to obtain the shirikodama. Kappa do not always kill for the purpose of touching or obtaining a shirikodama. They lurked in toilets that were over rivers for the sole purpose of sexually assaulting women. It was not uncommon for these women to later give birth to a Kappa child. Upon birth these children were cut into pieces and buried in jars because of their hideous appearance.

There are some mummified remains purportedly belonging to a Kappa, including a foot and an arm with a hand attached. The remains were given to the Miyakonijo Shimazu family after a Kappa was supposedly shot on a riverbank in 1818.

There was an incident in 1991 where a Japanese male teacher witnessed the scene of a Kappa appearing in the water with his own eyes. He also photographed it with his own camera. At the time, the children of Tobuchi Elementary School in Noichi, Iwate Prefecture, led by Mr. Tori Segawa, suddenly saw an unidentified creature moving in the river. It looked like a Kappa. Its body was dark green, with scaly skin, no hair, and a pointed mouth.

In June 1991, there was another sighting of a Kappa in Miyazaki Prefecture by a local resident named Matsumoto. After shopping and returning home, he smelled a strong stench. Matsumoto responded, a thief entered the room, but after checking everything, nothing was missing. He did find strange footprints that were about twelve centimeters long with only three toes in a shape similar to webbing in the middle of each toe. These creatures are also in China and other parts of Asia. The Kappa is an interesting creature, but on to the Almas.

ALMAS

The Almas is a small bipedal Bigfoot-type creature the ranges from Mongolia, Turkey, Bulgaria, Russia, Georgia, Kazakhstan, Tajikistan, Armenia, China, Azerbaijan, and Kyrgyzstan. They live in mountainous areas. They walk on two legs, are five to six and a half feet tall, and are covered with reddish-brown hair, with anthropomorphic facial features, including a pronounced brow ridge, a flat nose, long arms, long fingers, and a weak chin.

Sightings and stories of these creatures go back several hundred years. Almas has appeared in a Tibetan medicinal book. This book contains thousands of illustrations of various classes of animals, all of which were living and observed in the area. Sightings recorded in writing go back as far back as the fifteenth century.

In 1430, Hans Schiltberger recorded his personal observation of these creatures in the journal of his trip to Mongolia as a prisoner of the Mongol Khan. Schiltberger also recorded one of the first European sightings of Przewalski horses. Nikolai Przhevalsky observed the animals in Mongolia in 1871. He noted that Almas are part of the Mongolian and Tibetan apothecary's materia medica, along with thousands of other animals and plants that are still alive today.

Ivan Ivlov observed, in 1963, a whole family of Almas. Ivlov, a pediatrician, decided to interview some of the Mongolian children who were his patients. He discovered many of them had seen Almas. The Mongolian children nor the young Almas were afraid of each other. Every country has a Bigfoot, but our next creature is a little different; let's take a look at the Buto Ijo.

BUTO IJO

The story of the Buto Ijo goes back ages to the time of nonconventional history. In these times Buto Ijo was a species of giant-kin who lived with their hearts driven by greed. Their greediness was their downfall. The king of the Buto Ijo led a raid on the Archdevil of Greed's treasury, and the Buto Ijo were defeated. The Archdevil cursed them to be his servants and were turned into fiends as their punishment for their incursion. Now, whenever a mortal asks for a fiendish pact to get riches, the Archdevil sends a Buto Ijo to do his bidding. The Buto Ijo is connected to greed and/or wealth. The story of Buto Ijo is a cryptid creature of Indonesia.

The Buto Ijo is very large and hulk looking, with green skin, black hair, protruding upper and lower fangs, and large round red eyes.

The Buto Ijo likes to kidnap children, bringing them back to their dwelling. They make the children their slaves, also using them as entertainment, and when they get bored, they eat the children. There are stories of the Buto Ijo, but no good stories of sightings, which could come from fear or social pressures. I have found that some of the creatures have a hold on people with fear and the repercussions of acknowledgment of their existence.

Now take a look at a creature that is paranormal and cryptid at the same time.

DJINN

There is a supernatural creature/spirit called the jinn or djinn within Hindu and pre-Islamic Arabian religious systems. It was also in Islamic mythology and theology. The jinn/djinn is an invisible entity that can be visible and can also change into human or animal forms. The jinn/djinn are not just evil or good; they can be what they want. Most people associate the jinn/djinn with genies. Don't count on running into a blue flamboyant singing genie if you come in contact with a jinn/djinn. I have found nothing that gives me any idea that they are that happy. However, in some of the cultures the jinn/djinn do come in colors. Some of them can be orange, blue, red, or even maroon. The Quran says that they are one of three intelligent creations of God. Angels created of light, humans created of dirt, and djinn created of smokeless flame. They are said to have free will, so that makes them unpredictable. They can possess people and animals, alive or dead.

Here are some encounters I found:

- A man went to pray Tahajjud at the mosque near his home, and while he was praying, he heard the door open, and someone came in to pray. He didn't think anything of it; as he went out, he saw only one pair of shoes, which belonged to him. He quickly ran back in, but to his surprise, no one was there.
- A man said his grandmother was on her deathbed when a cat started to appear in the house. The cat even appeared in the house when all the doors and windows were closed. It had a bad smell and was very dirty. When someone would recite a holy verse from the Quran, the cat would vanish. After his grandmother passed away, the cat appeared a few more times, and when it did, everyone would get sick.
- A lady decided to take a nap, and lay down in her bed. While lying on her side, she suddenly felt someone lie down beside her. She rolled over to find what was shaped like a man beside her. When she tried to move, she couldn't. She began to recite verses from the Quran. In a blink of an eye, the figure was gone, and she was able to move.
- A lady was sitting in her room in the evening when suddenly all the windows in the house started forcibly shaking. There was no wind outside. She rushed into the next room where her father was; he was a man of great faith. He looked at her

and told her not to worry; the spirits outside wanted to come in but could not.

These malevolent creatures play pranks, scare, and even protect. There is a story about people being protected by them, even an entire village that was protected by them. Now to the river serpent.

PHAYA NAGA

The Phaya Naga are mythical serpent like creatures that are believed to live in the Mekong River. People in both Laos and Thailand attribute the Naga fireballs to the Phaya Naga. Folklore says the creature is a semi-divine creature or demi-creature that possesses supernatural powers as described by the Buddhist and Hindu religions. The Phaya Naga is a cross between a giant snake and a dragon. The creature has red, green, yellow, and even golden scales, sharp teeth, a finlike tail, a giant horn on its head, and a collar with some sort of gem in it around its neck. The Phaya Naga has supernatural powers, like summoning rain or breathing fire. It is also said to signal the return of Buddha by blasting fire into the sky.

No sightings were found, but they were referred to as fake sightings being oarfish or an elongated fish with red crests.

Now from a serpent to horsemen.

TIKBALANG

The Tikbalang is a very unusual creature from Philippine folklore that in some ways reminds me of the Jersey Devil. The

Tikbalang is said to be a bipedal horse creature. It is a tall, bony humanoid creature, with a horse head and hooves, along with disproportionally long limbs. The form traces back over four thousand years, with roots in Hinduism.

Ancient people in the Philippines believed in animism. They believed that the world had its own consciousness and that stones, trees, mountains, water, animals, the sun, and the moon had a hidden power known as the spirit or idol. Tikbalang is known to be a bizarre, shape-shifting, trickster spirit that haunts certain places in the wildlands. They dwell in the mountains and forest.

There were some encounters, but I was unable to make sense of them. Some would not translate, and therefore, I could not read them.

MANTICORE

Here is one of the wildest creatures in history, the manticore. The manticore is a legendary Persian creature similar to the

Egyptian sphinx that proliferated in western European medieval art as well. It has the head of a human, the body of a lion, and a tail of venomous spines. Some versions have the tail as a scorpion's tail. Some accounts compare the spines to arrows.

It was first mentioned as far back as 404–359 BC. I found no sightings or encounters. There was one video that was supposed to be of a manticore, but it was a bad computer-generated video.

On to the rock apes of Vietnam.

ROCK APES

"Rock ape" was the name given to a creature that was spotted and encountered by multiple American soldiers. The locals referred to these creatures as jungle people. The jungle people were bipedal, six to seven feet tall, stoutly built, very muscular, with protruding stomachs, and were covered in hair, either black or brown, with no hair on their knees, the soles of their feet or face. The jungle people tended to live in isolated, remote areas of the jungle. The people who mistakenly cross the path of the jungle people pay a price. The jungle people become bold and very aggressive, and they don't hesitate to attack. The jungle people are most active at dusk or in the dark, and they travel in packs or groups.

Here are some of the encounters with the rock apes.

Here is a story from six men of the 101st Airborne Division. The unit was resting when about fifteen yards uphill, a tree suddenly began to shake violently. The soldiers prepared for what they believed to be the enemy coming through the trees. But as they watched the trees, they saw something unusual. It was a creature with an oblong head with reddish hair, a huge mouth, and dark deep-set eyes emerging from the bush. It stood right in front of them in a clear area. The creature was about five feet tall and was very muscular with matted red hair. The creature stood on two legs and examined the soldiers as they examined it. The soldiers argued back and forth on whether it was or was not an orangutan. Then it retreated into the jungle.

Another incident occurred in 1966 on hill 868 in Quang Nam Province. A Marine unit was reporting to their captain that they had spotted movement in the brush, which they assumed was the Viet Cong. The captain told his unit over the radio not to fire. Soon after, the unit reported back that rather than the Viet Cong, they were being surrounded by hairy, bipedal humanoid creatures. The captain told the unit not to fire on the creatures, instead just throw rocks at them. To their surprise, the creature threw the rocks back at them. The Marines realized that hundreds of the creatures had started moving on them, so they moved from the area.

From jungle people to a giant.

GIANT OF KANDAHAR

Illustrated by
Nate Hallinan

I n 2002 in the Kandahar region of Afghanistan, an infantry group went missing. The odd thing was there was no communication before they went missing. A Navy SEAL team was sent in to investigate what had happened to the infantry group. The SEAL team was dropped into enemy territory.

After two days, the team found a goat trail and decided to follow it up to the plateau. When they arrived, they saw a very large opening with bones all around in front. One of the SEALs saw a piece of communications equipment that belonged to the missing unit. The team realized that it could be an ambush, and they took positions to prepare for the ambush, when suddenly something that no one could prepare for happened. A huge wooden spear came out of the cave like a missile, hitting one of the SEALs. The SEALs all saw their teammate who was struck by this wooden spear die. A giant human creature burst out of the cave with incredible speed, grabbing its spear. Seeing this twelve-to-fourteen-foot human creature dressed in animal skins—with six fingers, six toes, flaming red hair, and two rows of teeth—turn towards them as it pulled the spear from the body of their teammate, the SEALs were in shock, but their training kicked in. The team opened fire with M4 rifles, .308 rifles and .50-caliber rifles. The giant was taking rounds but was still trying to go after them when one of the SEALs yelled, "Shoot his face!" They all rotated their fire to the head and face. It only took thirty seconds from the start to the end when the giant fell dead. The SEALs called in for extraction; two helicopters came in and picked up the SEALs in one and the giant in the other.

At the debrief they were told not to speak of this, and the giant was removed from the country in a C-130.

From a giant to the yeti.

YETI

Now let's talk about the yeti. There are other names for the yeti, but the most famous name is abominable snowman. The creature wanders from the Himalayan Mountains through Bhutan, China, India, Napal, and Russia. The yeti is six feet tall to around eight feet tall in most cases, with a range of colored fur from brown, black, reddish, gray, and yes, even white.

The yeti runs deep in history; even Alexander the Great demanded to see a yeti when he conquered the Indus Valley in 326 BC. The local people told him they were not able to present him one because the creature could not survive at that low an altitude. In 1921, a journalist named Henry Newman interviewed a group of British explorers who had just returned from Mount Everest. The explorers explained that they had discovered some very large footprints on the mountain, which their guides had attributed to "metoh-kangmi," basically meaning "man-bear snow-man." But when the first part of the translation was botched, the word "metoh" was wrongly translated as "abominable." That is how we got the name abominable snowman.

In 1942, two hikers saw two black specks moving across the snow about a quarter mile below them. They gave a very descriptive report of what they saw. The height was not much less than eight feet tall, their heads were squarish, and the ears lay close to their skulls. The shoulders sloped down to a powerful chest. The creatures were covered in reddish brown hair, which formed a close-body fur mixed with long straight hairs hanging downward. Another person saw a creature about the size of a man, the head covered with long hair, but the face and chest were not very hairy at all. Reddish-brown in color and bipedal, it was busy grubbing up roots and occasionally emitted a loud high-pitched cry. Tracks in the snow have been found, but some of the tracks were actually rock or snow falling down the mountain and bouncing. The sherpas have tales of the yeti attacking people, and the Buddhist and Hindu say they are good and even guardians. The yeti is steeped in legend; they go back to the beginning of time.

THE GOLEM

The golem is very different than any other cryptids. The golem is not a natural creature; they are created by a person from mud or clay. Golems are animated anthropomorphic beings in Jewish folklore. The golem is the size of an average person and can only be brought to life by a divine person like a rabbi. Golems are talked about in the Talmud where Adam was referred to as starting off as a golem because he was created from mud. No golem is fully human. One main disability of a golem was its inability to speak.

During the Middle Ages, passages from the Sefer Yetzirah (book of creation) were studied as a means to create and animate a golem, although there is little in the writings of Jewish mysticism that supports this belief. There is a belief that golems might be activated by an ecstatic experience induced by ritualistic use of various letters of the Hebrew alphabet forming a "shem" (any one of the Names of God). The shem was written on a piece of paper and inserted into the mouth or forehead of the golem.

A golem is inscribed with Hebrew words in some tales. The Hebrew word for truth is put on the forehead to bring the golem to life, and some is rubbed off to stop the golem.

In the eleventh century, Solomon ibn Gabirol created a female golem to do housework. There are stories throughout history of golems being brought to life for different tasks. It was even said that a golem was created to protect the Jewish ghettos.

I wanted to include sightings of golems, but I could not find any credible-sounding sightings, and the videos I found looked like some bad photoshopped stuff.

Our last Asian creature is the Manananggal.

MANANANGGAL

T he Manananggal is a vicious, vampire-like creature that originated in the Philippines. It is a human eater and blood-sucker. It looks like a disgusting, hideous woman. It has the ability to sever its upper torso from its lower torso while sprouting batlike wings. It uses the wings to fly through the air and look for its next victim. When it flies up after the body separates and the wings form, it leaves the intestines trailing behind.

The creature primarily preys on pregnant women in the middle of the night when they sleep. It uses its elongated tongue to suck out the woman's blood or the heart of the fetus. When the creature chooses a man for its prey, it can appear as a beautiful woman. It will then lure the man to a private place where it attacks and eats the victim alive, focusing on the stomach, heart, and liver.

The Manananggal can only be killed when the sunlight hits its separated torso. You can put salt or garlic on the lower half of the separated torso, preventing it from joining back together. The creature has to be whole when the sun rises. Some people believe a black chick lives inside the creature and eats the innards of the creature while keeping it alive. While others believe you can turn into a Manananggal by chanting a special incantation, anointing yourself with oil, and procuring an egg that contains a black chick.

The creatures are commonly accompanied by a tiktik bird. The bird's calls assist the creature and confuse its victim. The Manananggal will fly to the house of its victim and land on the roof, looking for a way to enter, but if you leave pots of uncooked rice, ash, or salt around the house, they may decide not to enter.

The Manananggal have wide eyes and wild hair. Its teeth can change into fangs, and its fingers can change into long claws.

Sorry, unable to find sightings.

Asia was cool; on to Europe.

Part Two

EUROPE

Here we are in Europe. I had the pleasure to visit some of Europe when I was in the US Navy. I also have a treat for you with this look at monsters of Europe. It will include four eyewitness encounters sent to me by some great people who have entrusted me to bring their experiences to you. Their encounters will be in their words, I do not change anything, so what you read is all of them. I am very honored, and I thank each of them for their story. On to Europe and some of the cryptid monsters that dwell there. We are starting off with the European version of the American jackalope.

WOLPERTINGER

The Wolpertinger is a creature that looks like a composition of animal parts. The head of a rabbit, body of a squirrel, the antlers of a deer, and the wings of a pheasant. The look may vary depending on where you are in the German and Austrian area. Wolpertinger is a shy, frugal animal that feasts on herbs and roots found only in the Bavarian Forest, as well as occasional insects. They are not dangerous to humans, but beware if its saliva touches your skin; thick tufts of hair will begin to sprout. Also be warned if the Wolpertinger feels threatened, it will spray a foul-smelling liquid like a skunk. Unlike a skunk, nothing will dull the stink, not even tomato juice; it will magically disappear exactly seven years to the day.

I looked up some sightings of the Wolpertinger, but this creature has a huge following, and that made it hard to confirm any of the sightings. The stories almost seem made up or fantasies. I did read one story of a lady on a morning walk who was said to have seen it on the trail, eating leaves. As she approached, it scurried off into the woods. These are small creatures, and I really didn't expect to get any real sightings.

On to our next monster, the Tatzelwurm.

TATZELWURM

The Tatzelwurm is not a sweet creature like the Wolpertinger. The Tatzelwurm is known as the Alps dragon and has been reported in every country that the Alps goes through for hundreds of years. The name of the creature changes in other countries. It is known as the Tatzelwurm, Stollenwurm, Arassas, Praatzelwurm, and Berstutzen.

The creature looks like the back half of a snake and the front half of a feline chimera, to something resembling a small Asian dragon covered in scales. The creature is venomous and able to kill a human instantly with its bite. Its breath is poisonous fumes, and its blood is like acid. They are around one to seven feet long. They are also said to have two to six legs.

The earliest documented encounter was in 1779 when two of these creatures appeared in front of Hans Fuchs. This scared him enough to cause a heart attack; however, before he died, he told his family about his encounter. Hans described the creature as five to seven feet long with a snakelike body, clawed front legs, and a large feline-like head with sharp teeth.

In 1828, a peasant supposedly found the corpse of a Tatzelwurm, which by the time he had managed to bring it home, crows had apparently eaten half of the creature.

A two-legged Tatzelwurm leaped nine feet in the air toward two witnesses near Rauris, Salzburg, Austria, in the summer of 1921. It was gray, about two to three feet long, and had a head like a cat.

There are other sightings and reports of remains being found. I believe that this creature is alive and still lives in the Alps.

BLACK SHUCK

Now we move on to one of the most famous monsters in England; the creature is the Black Shuck. Black Shuck, or Old Shuck, is said to be a very large wolf with red eyes. You may be thinking people are just seeing a wolf or maybe a coyote. Well, you would be right, but wolves went extinct in the eighteenth century, and there are no coyotes in England. Now there is a chance that there is a small population of wolves in England, but I doubt it because of the size of England

and the number of people who live there. The Shuck is always black. Black wolves are few and far between, even with a big population. Black Shuck is said to be a supernatural creature.

The legend says on Dartmoor in southern Devon, the notorious squire Richard Cabell was said to have been a huntsman who sold his soul to the Devil. When he died in 1677, black hounds are said to have appeared around the burial chamber. The ghostly huntsman is said to ride with black dogs; this tale inspired Arthur Conan Doyle to write his well-known story *The Hound of the Baskervilles*.

Black Shuck has even been said to be a hellhound. We are lucky because I have a real encounter with a good man named Jonny Elliott. Now, he refers to the creature as a dogman, but after reading his story and hearing his interview (I included the Youtube link to his interview), I am convinced he saw one of the most incredible creatures in the world. Here it is:

JONNY ELLIOTT

I'm from the UK, a place called Ashton under lyne Manchester. The encounter I had was a few years ago. The cryptid I saw was a Dogman on a place called heart shed pike. So it was a summer night here in the UK, I was walking on the main road called Mosley road when in the Conner of my eye, I saw this dark mass, at first I thought it was an oversize dog but then I noticed it had red eyes and I thought, this no dog and we made full eye contact. Then I release it's no dog it's more like a wolf, then I thought there no wolfs wild in this country so I carry on walking.

Jonny Elliott had an amazing encounter, and he has a group there in the UK to investigate cryptid creatures. Check him out online: https://youtu.be/YpKby4uovzU

BASILISK

The basilisk appeared in many forms throughout history. It began as a small, crowned snake creature able to kill with a lethal poison and an evil gaze. The poison was so lethal it left a wide trail of venom in its wake. Despite its cruel nature, it still represents power;

thus it became the guardian creature and the symbol of the Swiss city Basel.

The basilisk is believed to be the most poisonous creature that ever lived, there are tales where the creature was killed by a spear thrown from horseback, but the poison sprayed up in the air, hitting and killing both the man and the horse. The basilisk presence is so tainted that plants die and rocks shatter. The venom is so strong that upon drinking from a well, the water remains polluted for centuries, killing anyone who drinks from it.

Medieval travelers described it as a large, fire-breathing creature with a terrifying roar. They described it as a rooster with a serpent's tail and dragon wings. The basilisk is hatched from a rooster's egg and incubated by a toad.

There are tales about the basilisk being petrified by its own appearance in a mirror; it is also vulnerable to the rooster's crow.

I found no sightings of the basilisk, so I guess they're in hiding or no one lives after sighting one. I will let you decide.

MAVKA

I know you must be thinking, a book of monsters and here is a lovely half-naked woman. But wait, appearances can be deceiving. This creature is a Mavka, which is old Slavic for the dead. These creatures are female, tall, round-faced, long-haired, and sometimes naked.

They are nymphs, which are the souls of girls who died from unnatural deaths.

They are believed to live in groups in the forest, mountain caves, and/or sheds; they decorate where they live with rugs. They make the thread from stolen flax and weave thin transparent cloth to make their clothes. They love flowers, which they wear in their hair. Every spring they plant flowers in the mountains, where they entice young men. Once the young men are under their power, they "tickle" them to death. Well, I guess there are worse ways to die than a half-naked woman tickling you to death. There are no reports of sightings, but who would know?

WIGHTS

I have to admit I was not going to put this creature in the book, but
I know there are a lot of *Game of Thrones* fans out there, so when I
found this monster, I put it in for you. The wight is a creature with

deep origins in European mythology, legend, and folklore. There are many versions of the name found in Scandinavian, Germanic, and English works. These creatures are fallen warriors and look like zombies. They are white skinned, very thin, with deep-set eyes, are very strong, and are smaller than the average human. They are the basis of the White Walkers in the *Game of Thrones*.

The word "wight" refers to an unfortunate "wretched" human roaming the world. They are known to congregate on the outskirts of human settlements. Wights are known to have unanimously sour dispositions. This may range from pitiful misery, to ravenous, to surly and hostile. They are driven by the instinct to feed on the living. Unlike zombies, they retain some rudimentary memory of who they were in life. Some of their abilities include being able to absorb the life force from their victims. Unlike zombies that eat you, these monsters absorb the energy that gives you life. They have no heartbeat or need of air to breathe. Removal of their head, like zombies, will kill them. I found no sightings, and to be honest, I didn't expect to.

NUCKELAVEE

The Nuckelavee is considered to be the most malevolent of the demons in and around the Scottish islands, without any redeeming characteristics. In the summer months, it was restrained in the depths of the ocean by the deity known as the Mither O'the Sea. It's a unique and solitary creature possessing extensive evil powers. It has the ability to influence events throughout the islands. Its breath is toxic and can wither crops, cause a drought, and cause disease along with plagues to livestock and humans. The Nuckelavee hates the smell of burning seaweed to create kelp. It will enrage the creature, sending it into a fit of rage. Once enraged, it kills fields of cattle. The only person who can stop him is the Mither O'the Sea.

Nuckelavees have a muscular thick build and stand nearly six feet tall at the top of the horse's head and around nine feet to the top of the human's head. It weighs in at nearly two thousand pounds. The legs have fins on them, and a single large eye burns with a red flame. The human head is large; the bodies of the human and horse are merged at the waist of the human and the back of the horse. The creature has no skin, black blood coursing through its yellow veins, pale sinews, and powerful muscles visible as a pulsating mass. They also have an aversion to fresh water. No sightings reported.

STRIGOI

T he strigoi come to us from Romanian mythology, and they are troubled spirits that have risen from the grave. They have all the same attributes as the classic vampires written in Bram Stroker's *Dracula*. These creatures are basically parasites feeding off the living. They have abilities like transforming into an animal, becoming invisible, and gaining vitality from the blood of their victims.

One of the first reports of a historical strigoi was Jure Grando

Alilovic (1579–1656) from the region of Istria. He was described as a vampire. Records refer to him as a vampire or strigoi. He was said to have terrorized his former village sixteen years after his death. Eventually he was decapitated by the local priest and villagers.

The most recent report was in February 2004 when a woman from the village of Marotinu de Sus in Dolj County revealed that she had been visited by her late uncle. Well, the problem is seventy-six-year-old Petre Toma died in December 2003. Fearing Mr. Toma had become a strigoi, the woman's brother-in-law organized a vampire hunt made up of several members of the family. After many drinks at the bar to boost their courage, they marched over to the grave of Mr. Toma, where they dug him up, cut open his chest, and ripped out his heart. After removing his heart, they burned the body; the ashes were mixed into water and drunk by his niece. The Dolj County police later arrested six members who participated in the ritual, charging them with "disturbing the peace of the dead." They were sentenced to six months in prison and ordered to pay for damages.

This action caused people in the nearby village of Amarastii de Sus to drive fire-hardened stakes into the heart or belly of their dead as a preventive measure to avoid the dead turning into strigoi.

GNOME

W hen you're talking about creatures in Europe, there are current creatures you are required to talk about, and well, gnomes are in this group. They're not mean creatures, but I have to put them in this book.

Gnomes are as old as Europe. They are said to be the first creature to live there. The gnomes average six inches (fifteen centimeters) up to about twelve inches (thirty centimeters), but with their hat on, they look bigger. They're pigeon-toed, which makes them faster and more agile in the wood and grass. The males weigh around ten and a half ounces (three hundred grams) and the females weigh a little less than nine ounces (two hundred fifty grams). The males wear a peaked red hat, blue or brown-green pants, and either felt boots or birch shoes or wooden clogs. Around his waist is a belt with tools, holding a knife or hammer. They have fair skin, rosy-red cheeks, and long gray beards. The females wear gray or khaki clothing consisting of a blouse and skirt. She also wears black-gray socks and high shoes or slippers. After she marries, she wears a green cap and braids.

Gnomes are seven times stronger than an average man and can run at speeds of thirty-five miles per hour. They also have better vision than a hawk. They eat what the forest provides, and they love alcohol. They play jokes on people, and sometimes they even help. There are many different kinds of gnomes, and they live in many areas in Europe. There are sightings, but I need to bring back monsters and get off these happy, helpful creatures.

LEPRECHAUNS

While in Europe we must talk about the most famous creature
in Europe, the leprechaun. These creatures are featured in

everything from movies to cartoons, to cereal, to toys. Most people don't know that leprechauns are not good or evil; they can be either depending on the circumstances. They dress in different ways, they are from two to three feet tall, quick-witted, highly intelligent tricksters, and will do anything to evade capture. They live in rural areas in Ireland. They make their homes underground, hiding the entrances as rabbit holes or in hollow tree trunks. They are said to hide their gold at the end of a rainbow. It is said that if you are very fast and lucky enough to catch a leprechaun, three wishes can be granted by his magic.

Leprechauns are happy creatures that dance, smoke, drink, and have been known to help people. But don't cross these little people, or they can be very evil. There are tales of leprechauns hunting people down who have done them wrong. Leprechauns are very strong, fast, and supernatural.

In 2020, there was a reported sighting of a leprechaun in the Irish countryside. Two teenagers and their little brother were returning from a walk in Cratloe Woods, County Clare, and recounted a meeting they had with a stranger in the ancient woods. The teens, along with their younger brother, were walking the family dog in the popular wooded area near Limerick. Mary O'Neill said, "We were out walking Gypsy, our golden retriever, when we came across this tiny little man (no more than three feet tall) with a big, long beard, and he was sitting on a small stone step while mending a pair of shoes. He was dressed in a funny sort of a top hat and knee-length breeches, and on his feet, he had the shiniest brogues I've ever seen. As soon as he saw us, he ran away, shouting, 'You'll never get me gold'; then he disappeared in a flash."

In 2009, the two hundred thirty-six surviving leprechauns in Ireland were afforded protection under the European Habitats Directive. According to the legend, they live at the Slate Rock below Foy Mountain, which is part of Cooley Mountain in Co Louth. As a mark of appreciation to the people of Carlingford for getting them protected as a species, the little people leave two thousand cauldrons for the streets of Carlingford for the "hunters" to collect.

I don't know if leprechauns are real or not, but I choose to believe they are, and they are part of the original inhabitants of Ireland. I hope one time to venture to Ireland to find out for myself.

BANSHEE

The banshee is another very famous creature that wanders the land in Europe. Banshees are considered to be a harbinger of death and doom. They are known by many names: Hag of the Mist, Little Washerwoman, and Hag of the Black Head, among others. She was a fairy woman, a spirit linked to the realm of the dead, and if you spotted her, you'd be praying for the safety of your family because it was likely that one of them would soon be joining her there.

The name "banshee" is from old Irish, for woman of the mound. Her name is connected to many different mounds of earth dotting the lands around the Irish countryside. The mounds are known as tumuli. These tumuli traditionally covered a grave or multiple graves, which are said to be the home of the spirits of the dead.

Little Washerwoman comes from tales of her being sighted washing the bloodstains from the clothes of individuals who were soon to die. Even if you didn't spot her, the banshee could signal her arrival by shrieking, wailing, or keening. Her shrieking is high pitched enough to shatter glass.

The first accounts of this creature date back to about 1380, and it is mentioned in some Norseman literature. There are also tales of a witchlike creature signaling impending doom in Scottish and Welsh mythology.

The banshee usually appears in three different forms. One is as a young maiden to lure people toward her with sweet singing, similar to that of the legendary Sirens, which drove sailors to crash their ships. The second is a full-figured matron or an old wretched crone. The third is as a white- or gray-cloaked female spirit with dark red or black eyes due to her constant weeping.

She is the predictor of death and would appear before someone entered a situation where it was unlikely they would come out alive.

There are old tales of battles being abandoned by soldiers because they believed they heard the cry of the banshee.

The first of all banshees, Aoibhell, was the queen of the Sidhe in the Province of Munster and was the guiding spirit of the Dalcassians, who become the mighty O'Brien clan, which was started by Brian Boru.

Aoibhell played a magical harp, and if you heard the enchanted sound, death was closing in on you. Cuchulainn himself heard it in battle and realized his life would be forfeit. The last appearance she made was to Brian Boru at the Battle of Clontarf, where his body lay dead at the end of the battle.

In 1642, Lady Fanshawe was a guest of the O'Brien family at their home, the Bunratty Castle. She woke up to find the light of the moon shining on a pale young female with red hair and red sunken eyes. On second horrible glance, it was clear the bedraggled wretch was floating at her upper-story window. The noblewoman stayed in her bed as the figure moaned in agonizing despair. The next morning Lady Fanshawe was told that a family member had died in the night.

The banshee was said to be a drowned servant girl.

PTERODACTYL

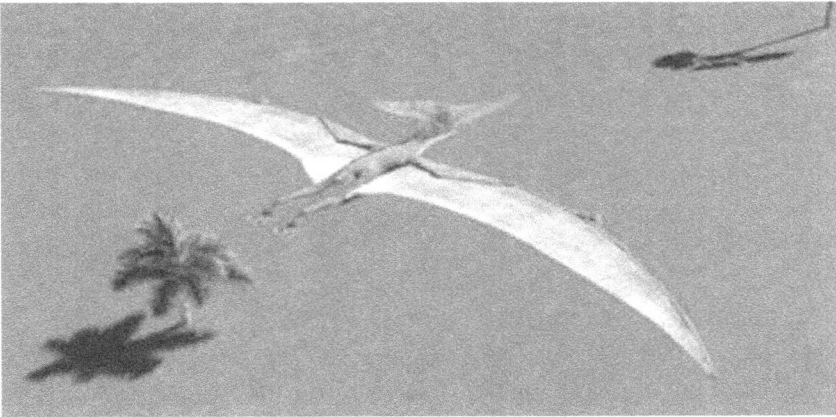

We have all seen dinosaurs in books and in movies. Pterodactyls had compact bodies, long necks, elongated skulls (which were created in some species), and had greatly reduced or absent tails. Pterodactyls' elongated beaks had about ninety razor-sharp teeth. They also walked on four legs not two. Pterodactyls flew the skies in the Jurassic and Cretaceous periods, but some say there are a few still flying around today.

In Kent, in 1963, four teenagers claimed to have seen a black bat with webbed feet, standing upright at a height of five feet tall, near Sandling Park.

Several pterosaur-like creatures were spotted at Hesketh Park, Southport, in 1999, according to claims. Ian Wharton, of the parks department, revealed how Clive Everson claimed to have seen a gray-skinned, bat-winged creature with a long beak and massive wingspan rise out of the bushes and fly away.

Once again, I have a treat for you. Here is an encounter for you sent to me by a man named Andy Booth. He had an incredible encounter, which he has given me permission to share with you:

ANDY BOOTH

So, at the time I was living in Milton Keynes, Buckinghamshire, UK. I would regularly go into my back garden and do some star gazing. If I stood in certain areas, the house and surrounding buildings and trees would block out 90% of artificial light, which is always a bonus.

This one particular night, think it was summer of 2014, I was out there looking up at the sky, probably around 11-11.30pm, I was facing the house probably about 8 feet away from it when I noticed something in my peripheral vision to my right. As I looked up to just above the top line of the house I could see this thing in the night sky, it was a full clear, cloudless night. Then I watched as it flew past, at a guess I reckon it was about 100 feet up and it flew in a completely straight line.

I continued to watch it without taking my eyes off it until it was out of sight, probably around 30 seconds, could have been less... Even though it was at night I could still see the color and shape and even some of the details to it. It must have been at least 24 feet long from head to tail and around 16 feet wing-span, it was a dark leathery brown color, I could see the hands attached to its wings, the same way that a bat has, even its tail had the diamond shaped end to it.

The strangest thing that stood out the most was that it didn't flap its wings, I didn't hear it make any sounds and it just pointed straight ahead without moving any part of its body, head included.

At first, I really believed I'd seen a dragon, so went straight on the net look-

ing, and did that for the next few months but came up with nothing. Even going out at various times of day and night to see if I could see it again.

It wasn't until about 3 years ago, I was looking on the internet and an image popped up (CGI or drawing), it was the exact same thing that I had witnessed, it was a PTERODACTYL!!! I couldn't believe that after all this time I'd finally found what it was I'd seen. It also proves that there are others out there seeing what I did that night.

Andy Booth

I want to thank Andy Booth for sharing his story with us.

LOCH NESS MONSTER

Once again here is another famous monster known all around the world. Yes, I know the picture above was a hoax, but it is the most recognizable photo of the creature. The Loch Ness Monster is better known as Nessie. The legend was born when a sighting of the creature made the local news on May 2, 1933. The newspaper *Inverness Courier* related an account of a couple who claimed to have seen "an enormous animal rolling and plunging on the surface." The story of the "monster" (the moniker chosen by the *Courier* editor) became a media phenomenon, with London newspapers sending correspondents to Scotland and a circus offering a twenty-thousand-pound-sterling reward for capture of the monster.

After the April 1933 sighting, the reports in the newspaper steadily grew, increasing more and more after another couple claimed to have seen the monster on land. Amateur investigators have for decades kept an almost constant vigil, and in the 1960s several British universities launched sonar expeditions to the lake. Nothing conclusive was found, but in each expedition the sonar operators detected some type of very large underwater objects moving around. In the 1975 expedition, using sonar and underwater cameras, they got a photo of something that resembled a giant flipper. The Loch Ness Monster is considered to be everything from a giant eel to a plesiosaur. There are no confirmed reports of what it is. I believe that Loch Ness has underwater tunnels that feed to the oceans, and the creature or creatures are moving in and out of the loch as they need to. There have been many hoaxes, but there have also been many unexplained sightings. I believe the creature is very real, and one day I will venture to Scotland and see for myself.

LESHY

The Leshy is a deity of the forest, which rules over the forest and protects it. A Leshy usually appears as a tall man, but he is able to change his size from that of a blade of grass to a very tall tree. He has hair and a beard made from living grass and vines. He is depicted with a tail, goat's hooves, and horns like Pan. He has pale white skin that contrasts with his bright green eyes. A Leshy has a close bond with the gray wolf and is often seen in the company of bears as well.

He is the forest lord and carries a club to express that he is the master of the wood. He has blue blood, which makes his cheeks a shade of blue. He has fiery green pop-out eyes. He also has no shadow. He is able to remain stealthy with the ability to change his size. He wears his shoes on opposite feet and backwards to prevent from being tracked.

Farmer and shepherds make pacts with him to protect their crops and sheep. The Leshy has many tricks, including leading peasants astray, making them sick, or tickling them to death. They hide the axes of woodcutters. If a Leshy crosses the path of a person in the woods, the person will be immediately lost and confused. The only way to counter the effect is to turn your clothes inside out and wear your shoes on the opposite feet. Leshies are terribly mischievous beings: they have horrible cries and can imitate voices of people familiar to wanderers and lure them back to their caves, where they are tickled to death. They are not evil but more mischievous. They trick people and kidnap young women; they are also known to keep grazing cattle from wandering too far into the forest.

So, in short, if you are in the woods, be respectful, and things will be good.

TROLLS

Now I know most of you have heard of trolls from books and movies. Big monsters that don't like humans, whether it be on

Harry Potter or *Lord of the Rings*. The trolls are beings of Nordic folk-lore, including Norse mythology. They are described as dwelling in isolated areas of rocks, mountains, or caves, live together in small family units, and are rarely helpful to human beings.

In later Scandinavian folklore, trolls became beings in their own right, where they live far from humans. They are considered dangerous to humans. They are much larger than humans, with a big nose, large eyes, pale skin, long arms, and are dim-witted. They have been known to eat humans. They hate every creature that is not a troll. I looked for sightings but had no luck. I looked at some so-called reports; they looked fake and so did the videos.

LAGARFLJOT WORM / ICELAND WORM MONSTER

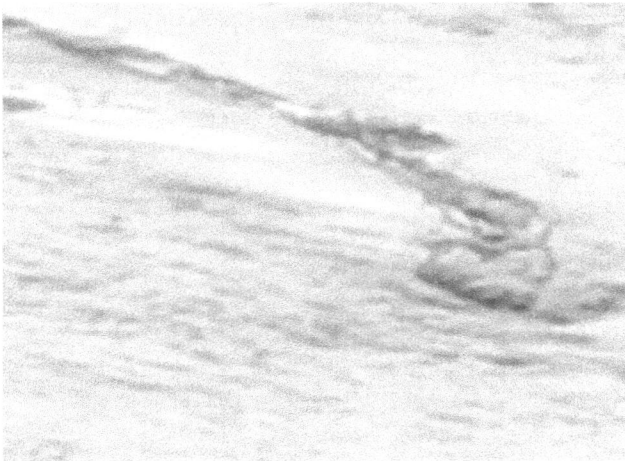

L agarfljot worm is a giant wormlike creature that lives in the Icelandic lake of Lagarfljot. It is described as being longer than a football field, two hundred feet long. The worm has many humps and swims through murky waters. It looks like a serpent moving under the water.

It has been reported coiled up or slithering up trees. The first reported sighting was in 1345, and its most recent sighting was in 2012, which either means these creatures have an extremely long lifespan (seven hundred plus years), or there is a small population living in the lake. There is also a legend that it was a lindworm thrown into the lake.

The story says: At one time, long, long ago, there was a woman living on a farm in the Lagarfljot district close by a stream where it broadens into a lake. She had a grown daughter. Once, she gave her daughter a gold ring. The woman instructed her daughter to catch a snake and keep the ring underneath it in her linen chest (according to ancient rural tradition). She did so, but when the girl went to look at her ring again, the snake had grown so large that the chest was beginning to come apart. Then the girl was frightened, and she picked up the chest with everything in it and threw it in the lake. A long time passed, and gradually people became aware that there was a serpent in the lake, for it was beginning to kill both people and animals that crossed the lake.

Once again, no legitimate sightings to pass on. There was one video redone in different videos.

BIGFOOT ENCOUNTERS IN EUROPE

As you all know, there are Bigfoot-like creatures all over the world. A male averages seven to twelve feet tall, and the females run from six to eight feet tall. They are covered with hair except on their face and hands, with five toes on each foot (unless there is inbreeding), five fingers on each hand, a very strong odor, and are very muscular. I have two sightings and one testimony to share with you.

Here is the encounter sent to me from:

RON COXY COX

Hi George, don't know if you're interested in non-visual experiences but this is mine. I have shared this with Deborah Lilith Hatswell and the BBR. I would have been 17 then and the friend 15. It would have been around September 1986 and me and around 15 others had been messing around a spooky house that was situated in a golf course just outside of town. It was around 21:30 and we were heading back to the estate we lived in, everyone else decided to walk the long way home by road but me and a friend decided to walk the towpath home and save around 20 minutes. We had hardly made 75 ft along the path when we heard a roar (I describe it like a cross between a lion and a bear) and just like Neil we felt this vibrate through us also. We never spoke but both of us took 1 more step, about turned and double timed it back to the group. We did talk about this when we were away from everyone else but were at a loss to explain it. This incident had a profound effect on me. I grew up playing by the river and all our teenage days and very late nights were spent there. However, following this I would not be there unless there was a large group of us. At this time, I worked in an industrial estate across the river and used to walk the towpath to get there—not after this. I actually walked to the other side of town and cut across rather than go that way in the early hours. It was a good few years before I would walk that path alone. Incidentally, a friend and his girlfriend had an experience at the same location a few years previous. They are reported to have seen large glowing red eyes up in the trees and then heard whatever it was jump to the ground and go crashing through the undergrowth. That area is a large swamp. Sadly, I never asked him about it as apparently, he would become aggressive and hostile if it was brought up. He took his own life several years later.

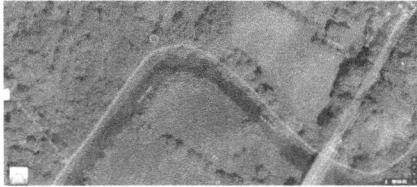

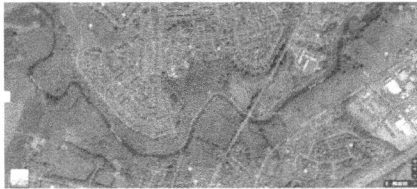

Location was close to Moore's Bridge on Hillsborough Road leaving Lisburn, County Antrim. The housing at top of overhead pics is Woodland Park and that on left is Old Warren Estate.

HERE IS THE SECOND ENCOUNTER FROM MIKE FARNELL:

My account happened in the summer of 1996 in a small village called Tarleton in the Borough of Preston northwest Lancashire. It began as a normal summer's day; I was 13 years of age, and I was out and about with a friend. We had decided to build an assault course through the local woods. Upon completing the course, we took a test run. We approached the end and noticed something vague walking toward us, in our child mind we expected it to be someone walking

85

their dog but as the vague form came into a part-clearing no more than 10—15 feet away from us, we were transfixed. It was a creature, 5.5 feet tall, covered in thick grey, auburn colored hair and had a huge muscular physique. We were in a state of shock. We looked at each other in disbelief and it was at that moment the creature growled. Fear took over at that point and I remember running as fast as I could to get out of the wood. From that incident I have never returned.

I want to thank **Ron Coxy Cox** and **Mike Farnell** for sharing their amazing encounters with us.

TESTIMONY OF PAUL GLOVER, BSC (HONS)

Matthew Johnson is crazy, delusional, a hoaxer, a liar... he is making all of this up in order to gain publicity. Back in 2015 that is the conclusions that I had come to and on his Team Squatchin USA Facebook group I had, like many others, I questioned his integrity publicly—I was subsequently kicked out of the group. The stories coming from SOHA were too farfetched and yet I had noted that Adam Davies had remained silent for a long period before coming clean that some strange incidents did actually take place at SOHA, backing up Matt's claims (although with different opinions). Listening to the podcast of Binnal of America on the 4th of October 2015 left me very, very confused. This whole Bigfoot theory had now been turned on its head... And meant, if we are going to progress with the subject, we should all have a bit more of an open mind. It was also at that point I started to consider the weird stuff that I had personally witnessed here in the forests of the United Kingdom looking for the forest people for myself. I had recorded stuff that I could not explain and yet all those years (50 years at that!) it was there already... recorded in the 1-minute footage of the PG film. Due to the painstaking efforts of M K Davis, he had, unaware of the significance, opened up Pandora's Box to the strange element of "woo" of Bigfootology... and yet here was Matt with the lid right open staring inside of it... Yet no one was prepared to listen to him.

My journey? I remember clearly when I saw for the first time a picture of Patty. I was about 11 years old, and we were on holiday in France and my dad had brought along a book by Arthur C Clarke about the world's mysteries... and there was a colour image of frame 352. My head was full of awe that such creatures roamed the earth... however, my fascination grew towards studying

Dinosaurs as I grew older. I went to Plymouth University to study Geology, and this led to me discovering a new species of marine reptile—an aigalosaur—the earliest marine ancestor to the T-Rex's of the oceans—the mighty Mosasaurs. Yet, I had not forgotten about Patty, the interest had never faded... it was just in hibernation mode. For a lot of people, they are unaware of their first encounter... sounds in the forest, distinctive smells, brief glimpses of shadows, sighting of large black cats even... and yet we are TOTALLY unaware. For me, it was when I was in my early 20s when I took my then girlfriend to a secluded forest lane to talk and listen to music—well away from any human contact and yet after a while I saw a large human figure standing 20 feet away behind the car. My thoughts were it was some kind of weirdo in the forest and reversed the car back and shone the headlights into the forest—Nothing was there. I thought nothing about it for 20 years, after all, this was the UK and not Northern California. I now consider that my first encounter.

*It was when I was around 39 years old that I saw Jeff Meldrum's book shortly after being published—*Sasquatch: Legend Meets Science*—the front cover picture was enough to demand my attention... so I purchased a copy from Amazon and read with keen interest the evidence, and scientific evidence at that, leading to the idea that frame 352 of the Patterson Gimlin film was most likely real and these Forest People do exist. I wanted to go to the USA and go and take a look for myself... and that's when the* Finding Bigfoot *series first hit TV. It was crazy... exciting... Scary... And fascinating all rolled up in to one... But such a shame it was all happening on the other side of the Pond. Or was it? I did some of my own research about reports in the UK, I bought Nick Redfern's books (which alluded to a green man spiritual element) and for fun, myself, my future wife, and my daughter went to a nearby forest and took a daytime look for ourselves. That is when the penny dropped that we were coming across structures that are seen across the US and Canada associated with Sasquatch behaviour and here—within a few miles of my own home! My quest for answers now had a secure hold on me... Every chance I had, I ventured into the forest and yet little did I know... I was being watched all the time. I had trail cameras failing, fresh tree breaks, new tree arches, trees pushed across paths—all recent activity of them, just like in North America. The more times I visited, the more times I found things. I then felt a pull to a different part of the forest that I would never have picked... And that's where my Bigfoot journey exploded. The forest people in the UK use ground sticks... something not* *explored very much in the US/Canada. Glyphs, tree arches and t-pee structures... all the same... but at this location there were ground sticks everywhere—over 1,000 in a concentrated area I would guesstimate. This was their home that they had drawn me to and my contact with them was starting to take on a new meaning. First contact was a stick broken off from a tree branch ten feet above my head (with an almighty crack) on a still summer's day and thrown at an angle right in front of my feet. My reaction was "I am dead"—I said some nice words and carried on and only about 50 feet away did I turn my back and looked behind me. Nothing! I left food gifts and then went home to calm my heart down. I returned a few days afterwards with the understanding that they meant me no harm. This was all good during the daytime, but what I really wanted to do was to do night-time visits, but I was too scared to entertain that idea knowing there are 8 to 10 foot tall forest people snapping trees like matchsticks out there. So overnight recording equipment was the start. I got a friend to visit too, who secretly labelled me as mad, but that was soon revised following our first night-time contact. This recording is on Youtube—where you can clearly hear bipedal footsteps and a crystal-clear strong wood knock (plus a lot more hidden sounds I have been told that even I cannot make out—like Bic clicks!). When you are in the middle of a forest at night in absolute darkness and just using your hearing as senses... that was my second heart stopping adrenaline rush. Lights on and we cleared out, yet we came back. My journey only got better from then on. A lot happened, we gained all sorts of evidence that science demands and yet the likes of Bryan Skyes and others, whom I approached, did not want to know (although only being just 40 miles away behind a desk in Oxford!). It was during those early days doing night-time visits that we started to witness light anomalies in the forest. When more than one person sees the same lights then you know it is not your eyes playing tricks with you. These light anomalies were orbs (sometimes very bright) just shooting through the trees. I can go on for ages talking about all the strangeness we had... so, I came to the conclusion that they mean us no harm so let's ditch the electronics and methods of trickery and let them approach us. And that's what they did... not only did they approach us, but they also visited us at home. How did they do this? Well... my TV would switch on at 2:22 am every time they visited. At first it was thought the TV had an issue... but it wasn't. The visits often occurred with lucid dreams about world events—most that had not yet happened. I had heard about mind speak so I tried to explore this and sure enough they were speaking back to me.*

Just for the record it should be noted that I understood that I was "sensitive" following a ghost hunt 10 years earlier where I was able, via meditation, to obtain the name and age of a girl who had died at Southsea Castle (on the English Southern Coastline) in the 1800s. She was the daughter of the light-house keeper who had fallen down a water well. I used the same techniques to make contact and confused at first, but I was getting messages back. I shared my experiences within a private Facebook group and was having a real hard time coming to terms with who the Forest people were. I was fully aware of Matthew's SOHA/SOIA by now and also Adam Davies and John Carson's testimonial, so I was sure that I had been wrong about Matt, so I took more of a keen interest in his experiences. My own contact with the forest people was getting more intense and this is when my contact with Gordon Dodds happened. He was a fellow Brit who had been to SOIA and had confirmed things. When Gordon returned, he was looking for open minded people to contact in order to open the doors to the Woo in the UK. I instantly got in touch with him... others took a more negative view of him. Enough said on that subject as that nega-tivity still reigns supreme here in the UK.

My mind had already been blown by what I was dealing with... but now I was climbing inside of Pandora's Box—the one that Matt had unleashed. My teaming up with Gordon was the start of an historical journey. It is now that I have to say that it is only through personal experience that your sense of reality is blown away. Our trips to the forest were experiences that I will cherish for the rest of my life. I started to see my very first cloaked sasquatch—where? Standing there—right in front of me! My eyesight isn't great so it took me time to adjust to seeing them... they can help from time to time by going from a shim-mering screen of glass to a smoky outline. They were there... not just one... but many. Red eye glow at low heights and yellow eye glow at 8 to 9 feet tall. Can my journey get any more surreal? Yes. My mind speak was getting stronger and I could happily receive communication during the daytime... but was best at bedtime just before falling asleep. Gordon had been told by Matt that he will have a guardian upon his return to the UK—and there he was—standing in front of me—his name Zameath. Gordon could not mindspeak with them, but he could see them much better than me... so together we had the abilities to have awesome night-time experiences.

I would like to add that around this time I had an overwhelming sense of guilt that I had in the past doubted Matt and had questioned his integrity publicly on his Facebook channel. I had to put the record straight and I openly apologised for my ignorance a couple of years previously. I was happy that he cordially accepted my apology and our friendship increased to a new level from that point onwards. I have the utmost respect for Matt. When the whole world is telling you that you're mad, delusional and a liar and you carry on beating that drum is the testament to the faith he had in his own journey. That was the cross he had to bear and knowing the Bigfoot world on both sides of the pond... to endure the ridicule and abuse you need to be a strong personality to take it and persevere. That's why the Xanue chose Matt and that's why I stand firmly by Matt in what message he and the forest people are trying to broadcast to us.

Getting back to the adventures that Gordon and I had... here, in the sleepy English Countryside. My mind speak had improved because of the contact I now had with Zameath and the clan that Gordon was involved with. It was great... I now sensed the difference between mind speak and my own thoughts going on inside of my head. I could also start to understand who was giving me the mind speak. Names had already come from my own contacts at the wood I go to—my contact was Zach and to be later told I had my own guardian called Sol. But... with the contact we had with Gordon's clan, we got to know the tall 8-foot-tall clan leader there called Ison. It turns out that Ison is one of the council of 12. Mind blown? Nowhere near yet... As we were making an effort to travel miles to each other's location... Gordon had a request to ask towards the Xanue. We wanted to know the name, the Xanue name, of Patty. Gordon asked me to ask my contacts and on the 25th, February 2018, I was given the name Enrith from Zach. I asked and asked again for confirmation and each time I was given the same name back again. This name was later confirmed with Steve Bachmann and his Xanue contact and with Matt through Zorth. To be honoured with now knowing Enrith's name Gordon dared to ask if Enrith would come to the UK and meet us at one of our joint visits. Because of the nature of this request, it took a few days before we had confirmation that not only will this event happen... but also, beyond our wildest dreams, each clan leader from the UK will attend this historical event, which took place on the 15th, March 2018. I had arrived late (due to new roadworks on the motorway) but we continued with the way we had proposed at Gordon's location. We were met at the car by Zameath and then walking down the wooded paths we were greeted by a host of others... lines of shimmering shapes... We then proceeded to our spot, and I remember looking up at the clear sky with Orion clearly rising above the horizon—it was a beautiful night. We then set up for the evening and I started to mind speak with my contacts. I was told there were over 500 clan leaders here from all around the UK. Were they all here? I was getting all sorts of ramblings going through my mind, seeing yellow eye glow... and seeing the odd shimmering image. Then down to business... Enrith had been wandering the forest and was just about to arrive... For this historic event I took a small dicta-phone to record our words. Gordon spoke out first... he had a speech prepared and from the heart he talked openly with Enrith and the clan leaders. It was well received. I then gave my own speech in recognition of my own personal journey leading up to this point. I offered my hand out to her and I received an electrical handshake in return. We asked if Enrith would show us some more just to confirm it was her and she responded by going a smoky grey. It brings a lump to my throat just thinking about this... And I do understand just how far from our reality this appears to be... I get that... alas, the truth will always be the truth and Gordon and I were there to witness this. We got messages and had a long chat about all manner of things... The significance of our event was the reason why all the clan members from around the UK had arrived. There were also members of the council of 12 there too. Am I and Gordon making this up? It is not in our interests to put our names out there only to be ridiculed—but hey—like Matt, we will keep beating that drum. Also, just for the record, Matt was asked following this if this had happened and yes, Zorth agreed this event took place. So... hard as it is... we are now aware of Patty's real name and that is something to celebrate. As you can imagine... our visits didn't stop... many more happened at both my own and Gordon's study sites—plus new ones that were encountered following this. I am sure Gordon has more words to say about this. And again, Enrith continued to attend the different meetings we had, even attending with family and other clan members from Bluff Creek.

We had only managed 2 overnight sleepovers in the last year, 2018... one was a bit of a wash out, but the second was awesome for me. Twice during the night, I felt my spirit leaving my body, being held, and pulled from my body by my forest contact—Zach and then being spun around at high speed before being carried off into the clouds and high in the sky and being taken on a tour around the planet—but at a supersonic speed. There is so much more I can say... but these are personal experiences which you can provide no evidence for. My journey continues... so, in summary I just need to underline that sometimes you need to experience things before your sense of reality is blown away. This is where we are now with regard to understanding the Sasquatch Forest people—the XANUE.

As for my acknowledgment to the work that Matt has done to date. I was once one of those ignorant flesh and blood missing link, ancestral primate researchers... But I was ignorant to a much bigger picture. Matt has shown the way. He is spot on... The forest people, the Xanue are indeed beings of light, inter-dimensional travellers. They can change their energy vibration so they can be seen and disappear—be seen on thermal cameras and as orbs of light. We have a lot to learn from them—so those who constantly demand a body or a body of evidence—you're going to have to wait. Get out from behind your computer screens and put the hours in so you too can experience the things I have. Learn from what Matt has been saying and show the respect to the people of the forest. We are on the cusp of a turning point in mankind's history... so, remember the lessons from Galileo before passing negative comments.

Location was close to Moore's Bridge on Hillsborough Road leaving Lisburn, County Antrim. The housing at top of overhead pics is Woodland Park and that on left is Old Warren Estate.

Thank you for your testimony.

HERE IS THE SECOND ENCOUNTER FROM MIKE FARNELL:

My account happened in the summer of 1996 in a small village called Tarleton in the Borough of Preston northwest Lancashire. It began as a normal summer's day; I was 13 years of age, and I was out and about with a friend. We had decided to build an assault course through the local woods. Upon completing the course, we took a test run. We approached the end and noticed something vague walking toward us, in our child mind we expected it to be someone walking their dog but as the vague form came into a part-clearing no more than 10—15 feet away from us, we were transfixed. It was a creature, 5.5 feet tall, covered in thick grey, auburn colored hair and had a huge muscular physique. We were in a state of shock. We looked at each other in disbelief and it was at that moment the creature growled. Fear took over at that point and I remember running as fast as I could to get out of the wood. From that incident I have never returned.

I want to thank **Ron Coxy Cox** and **Mike Farnell** for sharing their amazing encounters with us.

TESTIMONY OF PAUL GLOVER, BSC (HONS)

Matthew Johnson is crazy, delusional, a hoaxer, a liar... he is making all of this up in order to gain publicity. Back in 2015 that is the conclusions that I had come to and on his Team Squatchin USA Facebook group I had, like many others, I questioned his integrity publicly—I was subsequently kicked out of the group. The stories coming from SOHA were too farfetched and yet I had noted that Adam Davies had remained silent for a long period before coming clean that some strange incidents did actually take place at SOHA, backing up Matt's claims (although with different opinions). Listening to the podcast of Binnal of America on the 4th of October 2015 left me very, very confused. This whole Bigfoot theory had now been turned on its head... And meant, if we are going to progress with the subject, we should all have a bit more of an open mind. It was also at that point I started to consider the weird stuff that I had personally witnessed here in the forests of the United Kingdom looking for the forest people for myself. I had recorded stuff that I could not explain and yet all those years (50 years at that!) it was there already... recorded in the 1-minute footage of the PG film. Due to the painstaking efforts of M K Davis, he had, unaware of the significance, opened up Pandora's Box to the strange element of "woo" of Bigfootology... and yet here was Matt with the lid right open staring inside of it... Yet no one was prepared to listen to him.

My journey? I remember clearly when I saw for the first time a picture of Patty. I was about 11 years old, and we were on holiday in France and my dad had brought along a book by Arthur C Clarke about the world's mysteries... and there was a colour image of frame 352. My head was full of awe that such creatures roamed the earth... however, my fascination grew towards studying Dinosaurs as I grew older. I went to Plymouth University to study Geology, and this led to me discovering a new species of marine reptile—an aigalosaur— the earliest marine ancestor to the T-Rex's of the oceans—the mighty Mosasaurs. Yet, I had not forgotten about Patty, the interest had never faded... it was just in hibernation mode. For a lot of people, they are unaware of their first encounter... sounds in the forest, distinctive smells, brief glimpses of shadows, sighting of large black cats even... and yet we are TOTALLY unaware. For me, it was when I was in my early 20s when I took my then girlfriend to a secluded forest lane to talk and listen to music—well away from any human contact and yet after a while I saw a large human figure standing 20 feet away behind the car. My thoughts were it was some kind of weirdo in the forest and reversed the car back and shone the headlights into the forest—Nothing was there. I thought nothing about it for 20 years, after all, this was the UK and not Northern California. I now consider that my first encounter.

*It was when I was around 39 years old that I saw Jeff Meldrum's book shortly after being published—*Sasquatch: Legend Meets Science*—the front cover picture was enough to demand my attention... so I purchased a copy from Amazon and read with keen interest the evidence, and scientific evidence at that, leading to the idea that frame 352 of the Patterson Gimlin film was most likely real and these Forest People do exist. I wanted to go to the USA and go and take a look for myself... and that's when the* Finding Bigfoot *series first hit TV. It was crazy... exciting... Scary... And fascinating all rolled up in to one... But such a shame it was all happening on the other side of the Pond. Or was it? I did some of my own research about reports in the UK, I bought Nick Redfern's books (which alluded to a green man spiritual element) and for fun, myself, my future wife, and my daughter went to a nearby forest and took a daytime look for ourselves. That is when the penny dropped that we were coming across structures that are seen across the US and Canada associated with Sasquatch behaviour and here—within a few miles of my own home! My quest for answers now had a secure hold on me... Every chance I had, I ventured into the forest and yet little did I know... I was being watched all the time. I had trail cameras failing, fresh tree breaks, new tree arches, trees pushed across paths—all recent activity of them, just like in North America. The more times I visited, the more times I found things. I then felt a pull to a different part of the forest that I would never have picked... And that's where my Bigfoot journey exploded. The forest people in the UK use ground sticks... something not explored very much in the US/Canada. Glyphs, tree arches and t-pee structures... all the same... but at this location there were ground sticks everywhere— over 1,000 in a concentrated area I would guesstimate. This was their home that they had drawn me to and my contact with them was starting to take on a new meaning. First contact was a stick broken off from a tree branch ten feet above my head (with an almighty crack) on a still summer's day and thrown at an angle right in front of my feet. My reaction was "I am dead"—I said some* *nice words and carried on and only about 50 feet away did I turn my back and looked behind me. Nothing! I left food gifts and then went home to calm my heart down. I returned a few days afterwards with the understanding that they meant me no harm. This was all good during the daytime, but what I really wanted to do was to do night-time visits, but I was too scared to entertain that idea knowing there are 8 to 10 foot tall forest people snapping trees like match-sticks out there. So overnight recording equipment was the start. I got a friend to visit too, who secretly labelled me as mad, but that was soon revised following our first night-time contact. This recording is on Youtube—where you can clearly hear bipedal footsteps and a crystal-clear strong wood knock (plus a lot more hidden sounds I have been told that even I cannot make out—like Bic clicks!). When you are in the middle of a forest at night in absolute darkness and just using your hearing as senses... that was my second heart stopping adrenaline rush. Lights on and we cleared out, yet we came back. My journey only got better from then on. A lot happened, we gained all sorts of evidence that science demands and yet the likes of Bryan Skyes and others, whom I approached, did not want to know (although only being just 40 miles away behind a desk in Oxford!). It was during those early days doing night-time visits that we started to witness light anomalies in the forest. When more than one person sees the same lights then you know it is not your eyes playing tricks with you. These light anomalies were orbs (sometimes very bright) just shooting through the trees. I can go on for ages talking about all the strangeness we had... so, I came to the conclusion that they mean us no harm so let's ditch the electronics and methods of trickery and let them approach us. And that's what they did... not only did they approach us, but they also visited us at home. How did they do this? Well... my TV would switch on at 2:22 am every time they visited. At first it was thought the TV had an issue... but it wasn't. The visits often occurred with lucid dreams about world events—most that had not yet happened. I had heard about mind speak so I tried to explore this and sure enough they were speaking back to me. Just for the record it should be noted that I understood that I was "sensitive" following a ghost hunt 10 years earlier where I was able, via meditation, to obtain the name and age of a girl who had died at Southsea Castle (on the English Southern Coastline) in the 1800s. She was the daughter of the light-house keeper who had fallen down a water well. I used the same techniques to make contact and confused at first, but I was getting messages back. I shared my experiences within a private Facebook group and was having a real hard time* coming to terms with who the Forest people were. I was fully aware of Matthew's SOHA/SOIA by now and also Adam Davies and John Carson's testimonial, so I was sure that I had been wrong about Matt, so I took more of a keen interest in his experiences. My own contact with the forest people was getting more intense and this is when my contact with Gordon Dodds happened. He was a fellow Brit who had been to SOIA and had confirmed things. When Gordon returned, he was looking for open minded people to contact in order to open the doors to the Woo in the UK. I instantly got in touch with him... others took a more negative view of him. Enough said on that subject as that negativity still reigns supreme here in the UK.

My mind had already been blown by what I was dealing with... but now I was climbing inside of Pandora's Box—the one that Matt had unleashed. My teaming up with Gordon was the start of an historical journey. It is now that I have to say that it is only through personal experience that your sense of reality is blown away. Our trips to the forest were experiences that I will cherish for the rest of my life. I started to see my very first cloaked sasquatch—where? Standing there—right in front of me! My eyesight isn't great so it took me time to adjust to seeing them... they can help from time to time by going from a shimmering screen of glass to a smoky outline. They were there... not just one... but many. Red eye glow at low heights and yellow eye glow at 8 to 9 feet tall. Can my journey get any more surreal? Yes. My mind speak was getting stronger and I could happily receive communication during the daytime... but was best at bedtime just before falling asleep. Gordon had been told by Matt that he will have a guardian upon his return to the UK—and there he was—standing in front of me—his name Zameath. Gordon could not mindspeak with them, but he could see them much better than me... so together we had the abilities to have awesome night-time experiences.

I would like to add that around this time I had an overwhelming sense of guilt that I had in the past doubted Matt and had questioned his integrity publicly on his Facebook channel. I had to put the record straight and I openly apologised for my ignorance a couple of years previously. I was happy that he cordially accepted my apology and our friendship increased to a new level from that point onwards. I have the utmost respect for Matt. When the whole world is telling you that you're mad, delusional and a liar and you carry on beating that drum is the testament to the faith he had in his own journey. That was the cross he had to bear and knowing the Bigfoot world on both sides of the pond...

to endure the ridicule and abuse you need to be a strong personality to take it and persevere. That's why the Xanue chose Matt and that's why I stand firmly by Matt in what message he and the forest people are trying to broadcast to us.

Getting back to the adventures that Gordon and I had... here, in the sleepy English Countryside. My mind speak had improved because of the contact I now had with Zameath and the clan that Gordon was involved with. It was great... I now sensed the difference between mind speak and my own thoughts going on inside of my head. I could also start to understand who was giving me the mind speak. Names had already come from my own contacts at the wood I go to—my contact was Zach and to be later told I had my own guardian called Sol. But... with the contact we had with Gordon's clan, we got to know the tall 8-foot-tall clan leader there called Ison. It turns out that Ison is one of the council of 12. Mind blown? Nowhere near yet... As we were making an effort to travel miles to each other's location... Gordon had a request to ask towards the Xanue. We wanted to know the name, the Xanue name, of Patty. Gordon asked me to ask my contacts and on the 25th, February 2018, I was given the name Enrith from Zach. I asked and asked again for confirmation and each time I was given the same name back again. This name was later confirmed with Steve Bachmann and his Xanue contact and with Matt through Zorth. To be honoured with now knowing Enrith's name Gordon dared to ask if Enrith would come to the UK and meet us at one of our joint visits. Because of the nature of this request, it took a few days before we had confirmation that not only will this event happen... but also, beyond our wildest dreams, each clan leader from the UK will attend this historical event, which took place on the 15th, March 2018. I had arrived late (due to new roadworks on the motorway) but we continued with the way we had proposed at Gordon's location. We were met at the car by Zameath and then walking down the wooded paths we were greeted by a host of others... lines of shimmering shapes... We then proceeded to our spot, and I remember looking up at the clear sky with Orion clearly rising above the horizon—it was a beautiful night. We then set up for the evening and I started to mind speak with my contacts. I was told there were over 500 clan leaders here from all around the UK. Were they all here? I was getting all sorts of ramblings going through my mind, seeing yellow eye glow... and seeing the odd shimmering image. Then down to business... Enrith had been wandering the forest and was just about to arrive... For this historic event I took a small dicta-phone to record our words. Gordon spoke out first... he had a speech *prepared and from the heart he talked openly with Enrith and the clan leaders. It was well received. I then gave my own speech in recognition of my own personal journey leading up to this point. I offered my hand out to her and I received an electrical handshake in return. We asked if Enrith would show us some more just to confirm it was her and she responded by going a smoky grey. It brings a lump to my throat just thinking about this... And I do understand just how far from our reality this appears to be... I get that... alas, the truth will always be the truth and Gordon and I were there to witness this. We got messages and had a long chat about all manner of things... The significance of our event was the reason why all the clan members from around the UK had arrived. There were also members of the council of 12 there too. Am I and Gordon making this up? It is not in our interests to put our names out there only to be ridiculed—but hey—like Matt, we will keep beating that drum. Also, just for the record, Matt was asked following this if this had happened and yes, Zorth agreed this event took place. So... hard as it is... we are now aware of Patty's real name and that is something to celebrate. As you can imagine... our visits didn't stop... many more happened at both my own and Gordon's study sites—plus new ones that were encountered following this. I am sure Gordon has more words to say about this. And again, Enrith continued to attend the different meetings we had, even attending with family and other clan members from Bluff Creek.*

We had only managed 2 overnight sleepovers in the last year, 2018... one was a bit of a wash out, but the second was awesome for me. Twice during the night, I felt my spirit leaving my body, being held, and pulled from my body by my forest contact—Zach and then being spun around at high speed before being carried off into the clouds and high in the sky and being taken on a tour around the planet—but at a supersonic speed. There is so much more I can say... but these are personal experiences which you can provide no evidence for. My journey continues... so, in summary I just need to underline that sometimes you need to experience things before your sense of reality is blown away. This is where we are now with regard to understanding the Sasquatch Forest people— the XANUE.

As for my acknowledgment to the work that Matt has done to date. I was once one of those ignorant flesh and blood missing link, ancestral primate researchers... But I was ignorant to a much bigger picture. Matt has shown the way. He is spot on... The forest people, the Xanue are indeed beings of light, inter-dimensional travellers. They can change their energy vibration so they can be seen and disappear—be seen on thermal cameras and as orbs of light. We have a lot to learn from them—so those who constantly demand a body or a body of evidence—you're going to have to wait. Get out from behind your computer screens and put the hours in so you too can experience the things I have. Learn from what Matt has been saying and show the respect to the people of the forest. We are on the cusp of a turning point in mankind's history... so, remember the lessons from Galileo before passing negative comments.

Thank you for your testimony.

Part Three

AFRICA

Africa is known as the mysterious dark continent. It is also the second-most-populous and second-largest continent after Asia. Now, you're thinking, what monsters could live there with all those people and creatures like lions, hyenas, elephants, rhinos, and the most dangerous of all, the hippos? Did you know that hippos kill as many as three thousand people a year? They kill far more than any other creature in Africa, even lions and the many venomous snakes. But there are other creatures that roam the lands and waters of Africa. So let's talk about them. First up is the Grootslang.

GROOTSLANG

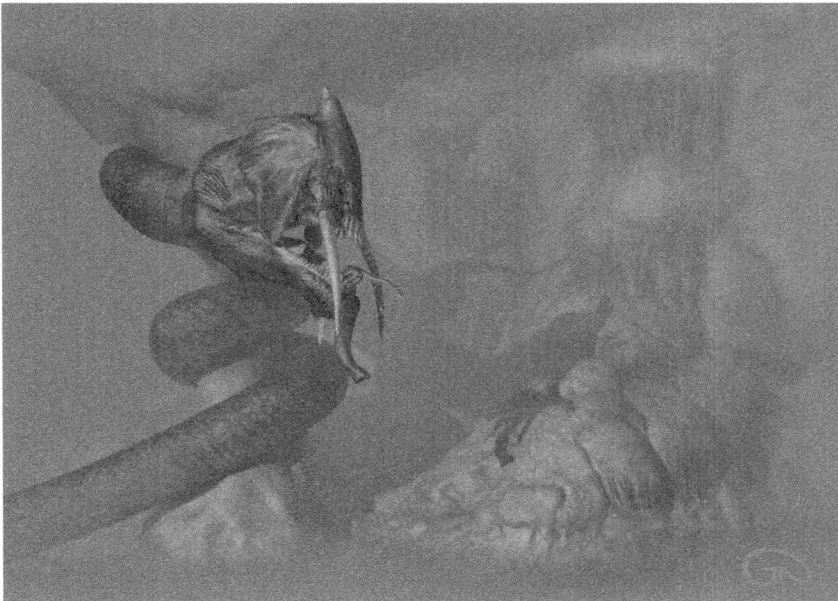

The Grootslang is said to be an enormous creature, an elephant-size serpent that lives in a cave in South Africa known as the "Wonder Hole" or "Bottomless Pit." The cave supposedly connects with the ocean some sixty-four kilometers, or forty miles, away. The legend says the lair of the creature is filled with incredible diamonds.

The legend of this creature goes like this: Grootslang is a primordial creature as old as the earth itself. The gods made a mistake in the creation of the Grootslang. They gave it tremendous strength, cunning, and intellect. When they realized what they had done, the gods split the Grootslang into separate creatures, and thus the first elephant and first snakes were born. But little did they know one Grootslang escaped. It was female, and she laid eggs, giving birth to the other Grootslangs, keeping the species alive. There are claims that the Grootslang lures elephants into its cave to feed on, but any animal or person could be its next meal. If you ever wander too close to the cave and this monster comes after you, rumors say you can bargain with it; if you have precious gems and give them to the monster, it might allow you to escape.

South African prospector Lieutenant Fred Cornell claims to have had an encounter with the Grootslang in 1910 and again in 1920 while prospecting for emeralds. On one occasion, he employed dynamite to dislodge the creature from a large stone in the Orange River, then shot at it with his rifle. Similar sightings continued into the early 1950s.

INKANYAMBA

INKANYAMBA
South Africa

There is a legendary aquatic cryptid creature that lives in the lakes and waterfalls in South Africa called Inkanyamba. This creature resembles a snake with a horse's head. It is most commonly seen in and around Howick Falls. Some say the creature looks more like a giant eel instead of a snake. The creature is over twenty feet long. Accounts of these creatures actually date back to aboriginal cave paintings found in the KwaZuluNatal area. These paintings depict creatures that archaeologists have come to refer to as "rain animals" due to their association with vicious summer storms.

As recently as 1998, residents of the Ingwavuma and Pongola regions of KwaZuluNatal blamed the violent Inkanyamba for a brutal storm in which thousands of people lost their homes. The ancient connection to the Inkanyamba and severe storms is due to the fact the creature is rarely seen in the summer months when it is very dry. It is believed that when the rainy months begin, the creature forms a giant tornado in order to find its mate.

In 1996, a local newspaper offered a reward for anyone who could produce photographic evidence of the creature. This drew photographers from around the world. Only two photos were published, but neither one gave enough evidence of the creature's existence. In May of 1996, the South African government was planning on capturing the creature and transplanting it into a protected area. Local Zulus were outraged by the plan, petitioning their local council for an intervention, but not for the reasons you may think. The locals were terrified that the expedition sent to capture the creature might not be ready to deal with the vicious disposition of the creature and that it could result in carnage spilling over into the villages. Reports indicate that the South African government reconsidered the project.

KONGAMATO

The Kongamato is believed to be a large pterosaur that is said to live in the semitropical regions of Africa. They are said to live in the regions of Zambia, the Congo, and Angola. Kongamato means "breaker of boats" or "overturner of boats" because the creature is known to attack fishermen by capsizing their boats, then attacking the fishermen in the water. The creature is a reddish lizard with membranous wings and teeth in its beak. The wingspan of the creature can range from four feet to one hundred feet across. The natives were shown pictures of a pterosaur, and they identified it as the Kongamato.

Scientists have found the remains of pterosaurs, proving that they once existed in those areas. The creature also resembles ones seen in Papua New Guinea and other places. There are several historical reports of European explorers being attacked by large-winged creatures that caused severe injuries. They are believed to eat mostly fish but occasionally humans. These creatures have even been seen digging up human graves to feast on the bodies.

Frank H. Melland talked to the native people and showed them pictures of a pterosaur, which they identified as the Kongamato. The tribal chief from the Jiundu region said that it dwelt in the Jiundu Swamps. Melland wrote of the Kongamato in his book *In Witchbound Africa* in 1923.

In 1928, A. Blayney Percival talked about finding a set of odd tracks, which the Kitui Wakama natives assured him were left by a nocturnal creature that flew down from Mount Kenya. Captain Charles Pitman recounted in 1942 that there were stories of a flying monster that dwelt in swamps on the borders of Angola and Zaire.

The first real sighting by a non-native took place in 1956 when J. P. F. Brown encountered two flying creatures with a wingspan of about three feet, a long tail, and a doglike muzzle on a road near L. Bangweulu, Zambia. They doubled back and flew overhead once more, and then Brown saw their sharp fanglike teeth.

IMPUNDULU VAMPIRE

They are said to come from the Cape region of South Africa, where the Impundulu vampire is bound to a coven of witches. The creature is only around three inches tall in its true form, but it has the ability to shape-shift. It stays in the form of a bird with a red bill. It spreads "the wasting disease," and it also causes infertility in cattle and men and also can cause heart attacks. At night it attacks both cattle and humans, drinking their blood and feasting on their flesh. A single creature can kill and consume an entire herd of cattle in one night. It revels in the pain and torment it causes.

The creature acts as a familiar to the witches and is extremely loyal by nature. The creature can be passed down from mother to daughter. The creature appears in its bird form while with its master.

I was unable to find any credible sightings, but with a creature that shape-shifts and kills, I didn't expect to.

ADZE

The Adze is a vampire creature from Ewe folklore as told by the people of Togo and Ghana. This creature is a shape-shifting monster, in the wild it takes the form of a firefly, but it can transform into a human. Be aware when it is in human form, it has the power to possess humans. Males or females possessed by an Adze are viewed as witches. The creature's influence would negatively affect anyone who lives near the host. A person is suspected of being possessed in a variety of situations, including women with brothers (especially if their brothers fared better than their own), old people (if the young suddenly started dying and the old stayed alive), and the poor (if they envied the rich). The Adze's effects are generally felt by the possessed victim's family or those of whom the victim is jealous.

In firefly form, it would travel through keyholes, cracks in walls, or under closed doors at night. Once it is in the home, it would suck blood from the sleeping people. Rumor is the people would get sick and, in some cases, die.

Once again, no sightings.

NANDI BEAR

The Nandi bear, or Chemosit, is a cryptid creature from the highlands of western Kenya in east Africa. It has been described as looking like a hyena mixed with a baboon. It is a shaggy, slope-backed predator, has a large head, a short snout, and is up to around four feet six inches to the top of his shoulders, and about the length of a lion. The color of the thick fur is tawny to gingery brown to dark brown. It has very powerful jaws that have the ability to snap bones.

The earliest reported sighting was made by a man named Geoffrey Williams and his cousin while on the Nandi Expedition to the Uasin Gishu in 1905. Williams did not report his sighting till 1912. He reported seeing a creature that resembled a bear, around five feet high, sitting on its haunches near the Sirgoit Rock. Before he could do anything, the creature got up and with a strange gait walked away.

There were sporadic sightings during the construction of the Magadi Railroad in British East Africa between 1912 and 1913 that introduced the Nandi bear to the wider world. The most famous sighting came from a railroad engineer named G. W. Hickes on the eighth of March 1913, at around 9 a.m. While traveling the railhead in a motor trolley, Hickes saw what was initially believed to be a hyena. Here is his report:

"It was on the line when I first saw it and at that time it had already seen me and was making off at a right angle to the line... As I got closer to the animal, I saw it was not a hyena. At first, I saw it nearly broadside on: it then looked about as high as a lion. In color it was tawny—about like a black-maned lion—with very shaggy long hair. It was short and thickset in the body, with high withers, and had a short neck and stumpy nose. It did not turn to look at me but loped off—running with its forelegs and with both hind legs rising at the same time. As I got alongside it, it was about forty or fifty yards away and I noticed it was very broad across the rump, had very short ears, and had no tail that I could see. As its hind legs were very shaggy right down to the feet, and that the feet seemed large..."

Hickes realized afterwards that the animal was the unknown "bear" that he had seen. He thought about stopping and following the creature, but people were waiting for him, so he completed his trip. He was going to return and investigate the tracks, but a heavy rain moved in and washed them away.

Sightings continued into the twentieth century. In 1914 it was reported one of the creatures had been killed near Kapsowar after it had killed several villagers. Another attack was reported the same year in an unnamed village in Kenyan, where a six-year-old girl was killed.

Colonial administrator William Hichens was dispatched to hunt the creature, and even though he had set up a perimeter around his tent, during the night an animal with "the most awful howl he had ever heard" ripped down the tent and carried off his dog, leaving behind enormous, clawed tracks. Hichens later wrote "sheer demonic horror" of the creature's howl.

There are other reports through 1958, and there were even expeditions sent out to find the creatures. Tracks were found, but the creature evaded being caught. It is believed to still be alive.

GBAHALI

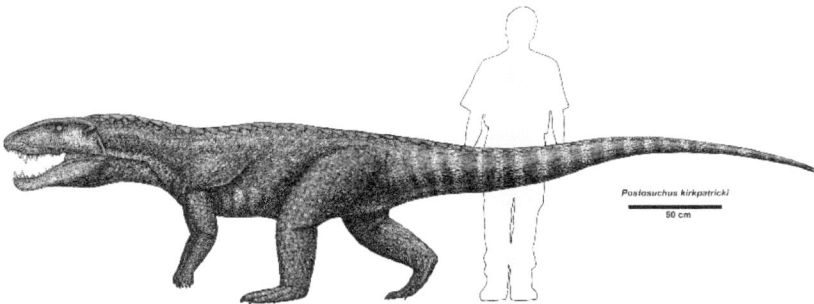

Postosuchus kirkpatricki
50 cm

T he Gbahali is a reptilian creature that resembles the extinct rauisuchian dinosaur *Postosuchus*. This creature grows up to thirty feet long, walks on land, is a strong swimmer, has powerful jaws, razor-sharp teeth, the front legs are slightly shorter than the back legs, and it moves very fast on land and water. The creature has also been called the land crocodile. Their skin is like armor, and it has three rows of teeth. They live and hunt in the rivers in Liberia. The Gbahali is an ambush hunter. It lies in wait, then bursts from the water, sinking its teeth deep into its prey, then drags it down into the depths, drowning its victim. It is said they drag the victim back onto the shore to eat it.

The locals have found ways to deal with the monsters. They use nets to capture the creatures, then blast them with shotguns.

John-Mark Shephard was an American who worked in Liberia with an international relief group. He sent a letter to a friend and detailed his experience and the actions of the villagers and their interactions with the Gbahali. He claimed that often villagers killed these creatures deep in the jungle and that the meat was sold to local markets. He also claimed that the locals built structures based on the length of a Gbahali carcass, and some villagers even claimed to have a skull of one of the creatures that was destroyed by rebels when the creature attacked the village. The creatures mostly appear in the rainy season, when they swim upriver, searching for food.

They have been known to kill people and are feared.

NINKI NANKA

Ninki Nanka

The Ninki Nanka is a legendary creature from the West African area. It is a reptilian that resembles a dragon. The creature is described as black and green, snakelike, with a feathery crest, and measuring about fifty meters (a little over one hundred sixty-four feet) long. It has been described in very different ways, one with legs like a lizard and, second, legless like a snake. Some describe the neck like a giraffe while others say like a crocodile. There is also confusion about what the body looks like, which ranges from a hippo and a dragon. The references say the creature can change itself like a shape-shifter.

Seeing the Ninki Nanka is almost a guarantee of death, or a serious illness followed by death. Some accounts also claim that death is assured if you lock eyes with the creature. Death can occur almost immediately to a few weeks apart.

The only thing that can kill the Ninki Nanka is its own reflection, and that is why the travelers along the river Gambia always carry a mirror on them.

In 2006, a team of dragon hunters from the CFZ (Centre for Fortean Zoology) went to Gambia to look for the creature. They were met with varying testimonies from individuals who claimed to have seen the creature or had an encounter with it. Eyewitnesses claim that it resembles a Chinese dragon and lives in the water.

POPOBAWA

The Popobawa is an evil spirit that allegedly thrives on the island of Pemba, near Tanzania. There has been mass panic over the years because of the Popobawa. It is a medium-size batlike creature with one big eye and reddish, leathery skin. Popobawa means "bat wing" in Swahili.

The creature is a shape-shifter and can take many forms besides a bat. It can take either human or animal form. It can metamorphose at will between any form. The creature typically visits homesteads at night but can be seen in the day as well. It is sometimes associated with the presence of a sulfurous odor, but this is not always the case. The creature is said to attack men, women, and children and may attack all of the members of the house before moving to the next house. Its nocturnal attacks can comprise from simple assault to sodomizing of adult men and women. Victims are often urged to tell others about the attack and are threatened with repeated visits if they don't. During panics about the creatures, many people try to guard against attack by spending the night awake outside of their houses, often huddled around bonfires with family and neighbors. Panics occur most often in Zanzibar, throughout the island of Pemba, and in the north and west of Unguja island, including Zanzibar town.

A peasant farmer named Mjaka Hamad claims he was attacked by the creature in 1997. In his words: "I couldn't see it. I could only feel it. But some people in my house could see it. Those who've got the spirits in their heads could see it. Everybody was terrified. They were outside screaming 'Huyo!' It means the Popobawa is there. I had this bad pain in my ribs from it crushing me. I didn't believe in spirits, so maybe that's why it attacked me."

MOKELE-MBEMBE

There is a creature that dwells in the Republic of the Congo and Cameroon and is said to inhabit swampy, marshy wetlands, lakes, and rivers. It is mainly around the Likouala region and Lake Tele but also seen in other areas. The creature is an amphibious animal with a bulky body, long neck, long tail, and a small head. It resembles a sauropod dinosaur. It could very well be a dinosaur that has been believed to be extinct but has survived in small family pods deep in the

Congo. The creature is allegedly ethnoknown to most indigenous peoples in the western Congo Basin, who give it various names.

The first report of the Mokele-Mbembe was in a book by Abbott Lievin-Bonaventure Proyaumes in 1776. According to Proyart, missionaries in West Africa reported the existence of a very large animal based on tracks that they discovered.

Here is their account:

> The missionaries observed while passing along the forest on the trail of an animal which was not seen but which must have been monstrous: the marks of the claws were noted on the ground, and these formed a print about three feet in circumference. The arrangement of the impressions indicated that the animal was walking, not running; the distance between the footprints measured seven to eight feet.

Another report from the German colonial officer Lubwig Freiherr von Stein zu Lansnitz, who in 1913 came out of retirement to lead the Likuala-Kongo Expedition to what is now known as the northern Republic of the Congo. Even though the expedition had to turn back, Stein sent his manuscript to German writer and naturalist Wilhelm Bolsche, who was working on a study of dragons. The study said that such legends may have been inspired by the historical survival of dinosaurs and other prehistoric reptiles. Bolsche subsequently included Stein's notes on the Mokele-Mbembe in his work.

Stein's description of the Mokele-Mbembe came from individual guides in the regions of lower Ubangi, Sanga, and Ikelembia Rivers, all of whom gave consistent accounts. Stein's original spelling, Mokele, has stuck. Here is Stein's manuscript translated by Bolsche:

The creature is reported not to live in smaller rivers like the Likualas, and in the rivers mentioned only a few individuals are said to exist. At the time of our expedition, a specimen was reported and from the non-navigable part of the Sanga River, somewhere between the two rivers Mbaio and Pikunda; unfortunately in a part of the river that could not be explored due to the brusque end of our expedition. We also heard about the alleged animal at the Ssombo River. The narratives of the natives result in the general description that runs as follows: The animal is said to be of a brownish-gray color with smooth skin, its size approximately that of an elephant; at least that of a hippo. It is said to have a long and very flexible neck and only tooth but a very long one; some say it is a horn. A few spoke about a long muscular tail like that of an alligator. Any canoes coming near it are said to be doomed. The animal is said to attack them at once and kill the people on board without eating them. The creature is said to live in caves that have been washed out by the river in the clay of its shore even at daytime in search of food. They are believed to eat plants only. The preferred plant as shown to me, it is a kind of liana with large white blossoms, with a milky sap and apple like fruits. At the Ssombo River I was shown a path said to have been made by this animal in order to get at its food. The path was fresh and there were plants of the described type nearby. But since there were too many tracks of elephants, hippos, and other large mammals of certainly.

There are reports of this creature as recent as 2021.

TOKOLOSHE

The Tokoloshe has other names like Tikoloshe or even Hili. The creature is believed to be a primate-type creature. It inhabits the nations of South Africa and Lesotho. The creature is able to move very fast even ghostlike. They love curdled milk. They have long, boney, withered fingers they use to choke their victims. They are said to be grayish in color, small, with a hole in their foreheads. They are said to look like a combination of a zombie, poltergeist, and a gremlin.

The story says they were created by a South African shaman who had been offended by someone.

There are beliefs that the creatures may also wander around causing mischief wherever they go. It is drawn to schoolchildren. The gremlin-like creature is supposably animated during a ritual in which a sangoma or African wizard/witch thrusts a hot poker into its forehead. The creature has another form of a bearlike humanoid. The creature has been known to disrupt communities and break up relationships. The creatures are known for raping both men and women, beating up people, and choking people in their sleep before stealing things such as clothing.

The only way to destroy a Tokoloshe is to find and destroy the muthi, which is the stuff a sangoma uses to create the monster. The muthi is made up of a selection of oils, herbal balms, and the body parts of animals all mixed together and buried close to the house of the victim the sangoma is after. You can protect yourself from the creature by putting a special blessed salt around the doorframes and window seals.

I am a little skeptical of the sightings I found. There are a lot of them on YouTube, but people can do so much with video, it causes me to not trust them, but they are fun to watch. I did not see any reports that I can verify.

DINGONEK

E arly European explorers ventured into the jungles in West Africa, where they found dozens of undiscovered species, which were confirmed, but they also brought back tales of bizarre creatures.

One creature was the Dingonek. Big-game hunter Edgar Beecher Bronson described it as:

> "Fourteen or fifteen feet long, head like that of a lioness but shaped and marked like a leopard, two long white fangs sticking down straight out of his upper jaw, back broad as a hippo, scaled like an armadillo, but colored and marked like a leopard, and a broad fin tail... Gad! But he was a hideous old hunter of a nightmare, was that beast-fish... blast that blighter's fangs, but they looked long enough to go clean through a man. A shot with a .303 caliber rifle only angered it."

It is a carnivore that is able to hunt and devour anything up to the size of an elephant. With tusks as long as a meter, very strong, and extremely aggressive, it is able to bring down a large bull hippo. The creature hunts using the ambush technique.

In 1907, famed adventurer and big-game hunter John Alfred Jordan reported seeing the creature and maintained his sighting to his death in 1933. Jordan described the creature as being about fifteen feet long, with scales on its body as well as spots like a leopard. He also described the head as similar to a big cat with long white fangs. It also utilized its tail to swim through the water.

Many tribes say they know of the creature. Some call it different names, like the Masai call it Ol-Umaina, and the Kikuyu people call it the Ndamathia.

AVIAN HUMANOIDS

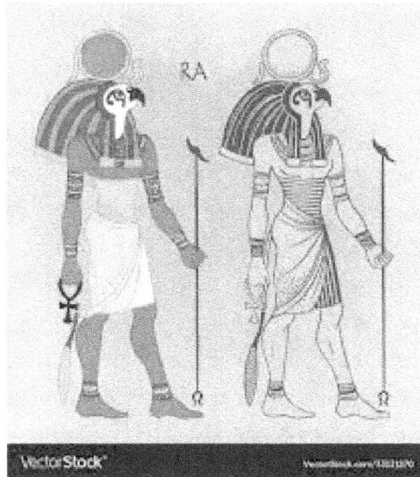

There are many versions of avian humanoids. Some are human with a bird head; some are humans with wings and feathers, a humanlike body but all bird features, and on and on. The creatures pop up all over the world. The Egyptians had Horus, Ra, Nekhbet, and Thoth, all gods with bird heads. These creatures appear to have been all around to world; they show up in Iran, Russia, India, Greece, and many other places. Some believe they are aliens and came here to help move mankind forward.

In 1962, on a deserted rural French road, a businessman claimed to have encountered a group of aggressive creatures that blocked his car and attacked him. In 1968 an encounter was published in the volume 14, number 6, November/December issue of *Flying Saucer Review*. The report came from a young researcher from South France named Lyonel Trigano. He interviewed an eyewitness who described what he witnessed:

"One evening in November 1962, I was driving along a minor department road in Var. It was a dark night, raining in torrents, so that I was driving with my lights full on." The trip had been thus far uneventful, but it would soon take a literal turn into the twilight zone. "Round the bend, I saw, eighty meters ahead, a group of figures clustered in the middle of the road. I slowed down to avoid the group, and at the same moment it split into two parts, suddenly and jerkily."

It was then he noticed something decidedly unnatural about the group in the road. "My window was down, and I leaned my head out slightly to see was a matter. It was then that I saw creatures, some sort of bizarre animals, with bird heads and covered in plumage, which were hurling themselves from two sides toward my car." He saw these creatures with full wings fly up and into a bluish UFO.

There are sightings throughout history all over the world. The Egyptians considered them gods. There are more sightings, and if these creatures interest you, go online; there are tons of sightings. If you're out at night, be very careful, or one may swoop down and grab you.

BOUDA

The creature Bouda is commonly known as a werehyena. This creature is very different than the werewolf. It is a shape-shifter; it can transform back and forth from hyena to human and back to hyena at will. These creatures are bigger than a normal human with incredible strength, speed, and intelligence. These creatures can be male or female.

In the former Bornu Empire of Africa, werehyenas were called Bultungin. Traditionally one or two of the villages were believed to be entirely populated by the creatures. In Ethiopia, blacksmiths were believed to be witches, and they could change into hyenas. The blacksmith werehyenas are said to rob graves at midnight.

In Western Sudan, the people believe that a hybrid creature that is human during the day turns into a werehyena at night. The cannibalistic creature terrorizes people, especially lovers.

The creature takes on the form of a magically powerful healer, blacksmith, or woodcutter while in human form. Some of the signs a human could be a werehyena are a hairy body, red and gleaming eyes, and a nasally voice.

They hunt in packs and are able to mock voices and use that ability to lure humans out where they attack and devour them. These creatures should not be taken lightly; they stalk, observe, lure, and attack.

Ethiopian Christians typically accused Ethiopian Jews of being the Bouda. They would spread rumors that the Jews would dig up Christian dead bodies and eat them. Jewish men in Ethiopian are often blacksmiths.

As you have probably already known, I have not found any sightings. I guess if you see them, they see you.

GA-GORIB

The Ga-Gorib is a troll-like gorilla creature that lives in caves on the sides of cliffs and in deep pits. These creatures are bigger and stronger than normal gorillas. They are aggressive and tricky. The Nagual or Vish Kanya tribes are said to feed their prisoners and criminals to them.

The Ga-Gorib is said to sit on the edge of a pit and taunt people to throw rocks at it, and when they do, the creature bounds to the person with extreme speed, grabbing them and throwing them into the hole to eat them at a later time.

This creature is very hard to find information on, and I'm not even sure it isn't something made up online, but if it is real, it seems very interesting. Also, no sightings, sorry.

Part Four

SOUTH AMERICA

South America is a unique continent. From the Amazon rain forest to the world's largest snake. There are many untainted indigenous tribes, hundreds of different languages, and it has the driest and wettest places on earth. It is also the home of the pink dolphin. This makes it a great breeding ground for unusual creatures. This is where we will start with the Alicanto.

ALICANTO

The Alicanto is a nocturnal, but luminous bird that lives in caves and mines in Chile. When these creatures come out at night, their feathers emit a metallic glow, and strange-colored light comes from their eyes. These are often depicted as a large bird, and the size would be an indication of the age of the bird. A full-grown Alicanto would be the size of a golden eagle or a giant condor. These birds are said to eat gold and/or silver, sometimes eating so much they can't fly. They build their nests near the areas where gold and silver, along with other precious stones, are located.

Spotting an Alicanto is said to bring good luck. If a miner can find and follow one, without being caught, the miner will find gold or silver. But if the miner is discovered, then the miner is forced off a cliff or lured into a deep ravine and falls to their death. The Alicanto have been known to help people if the humans share their finds with the birds.

I was unable to find sightings of the birds, but no one will report seeing them because it would give away the area with gold or silver. If I saw one, I would keep it to myself and get rich off the food of the birds while sharing it with them.

EL CUERO

El Cuero is a large, extremely dangerous lake monster. The name of the creature means hide or leather; that is because the creature has the appearance of a cow. The creature resembles a large primitive stingray, with a flat body, a long whipping tail, no barb, the eyes are on stalks, and the mouth is extendable like that of a sturgeon. Eyewitnesses have also reported seeing razor-sharp claws along the fringes of El Cuero that it uses to secure its prey. It is even believed that the creature is able to use hunting knives taken from their previous prey. The creature seems to be from two to five feet wide and weighs around sixty-five pounds. The creature is believed to live in the Chilean glacial Lake Lacar in the Andes Mountains. They have also been reported in rivers and lagoons in Argentina and Chile

El Cuero is an ambush hunter; it sits in the water, waiting for its prey to come to the water's edge. When the prey starts getting water, the creature surges out of the lake, and it uses its proboscis to puncture the skin and suck out the internal organs and blood.

There is an encounter where a woman came down to the river to wash clothes and laid her baby down beside her as she started to work. She was bent over washing clothes when suddenly the creature burst out of the water, landing on her baby, and then disappeared back into the water with her baby, never to be seen again.

CURUPIRA

The Curupira is a boy with red hair who is the protector of the forest in Brazil. The boy is short in stature, his feet are backwards, his skin is black or greenish, and the creature has special abilities to use to protect the forest and the creatures of the forest.

The Curupira uses scary whistles to leave a person feeling dizzy, sluggish, and with headaches. This trick ends up leaving the victim lost and unable to find their way back home. His feet are backward so as to confuse anyone who chases him. He uses the tricks to scare off hunters and woodcutters or anyone who enters the forest to do anything he considers bad to the forest. But beware, there are stories that he uses his tricks to molest virgin women.

No sightings are reported, but that makes sense with the tricks the creature can use.

MAPINGUARI

The legend of the Mapinguari or Mapinguary says he was believed to have been an Amazonian shaman who found the key to immortality thousands of years ago. His actions made the gods angry, so they severely punished him for his heresy. He was forced to transform into a wandering hairy beast for the rest of his life.

There are differences between the older sightings and the more recent sightings. Modern sightings describe the beast as looking like a giant ground sloth, whereas the older sightings describe it as more apelike. The creature has a horrid odor, which is so bad it can knock a man unconscious. It's said to be a humanoid monster with an eye in its stomach, one eye in its head, long very sharp claws, caiman skin, and backward feet. In the old sightings it is a primate, with thick dark hair, bipedal, and very agile. If the creature is startled, it shows its claws and is said to emit an extremely foul odor from its stomach.

In 1993 David Oren pieced together a description of the creature based on interviews with a number of claimed eyewitnesses. They described the creature as a man-sized animal, around a meter and eighty centimeters long, with long reddish hair, backward feet, and a monkey-like face.

The creature feeds on vegetation, including bacaba and babassu palms, which it twists to the ground and tears apart in order to feed on the palm heart and berry-like fruits. In southern Brazil and Paraguay, the Mapinguari is blamed for periodically killing vast herds of cattle by ripping out their tongues. The creature is said to have two very different vocalizations, one is a low call reminiscent of thunder, and the second is a very high-pitched cry.

One of the sightings comes from a member of the Karitiana tribe. Geovaldo Karitiana recounted his story to the *New York Times*. He said he was out hunting in the forest near what the tribe refers to as "the cave of the mapinguary." He's quoted as saying, "It was coming toward the village and was making a big noise... It stopped when it got near me, and that's when the bad smell made me dizzy and tired. I fainted, and when I came to, the mapinguary was gone."

TITANOBOA

The largest known snake is the green anaconda, which reaches up to twenty-five feet long and weighs up to five hundred fifty pounds. But for over a hundred years, explorers and natives in the Amazon have reported seeing snakes fifty to one hundred fifty feet long, weighing as much as five tons.

A British explorer named Percy Fawcett reported killing a sixty-two-foot-long anaconda. His claim received a lot of ridicule although eventually cryptozoologist Bernard Heuvelmans came to his defense and said that Percy Fawcett's claim was honest and reliable. Here is his account:

> "We were drifting easily along on the sluggish current not for far below the confluence of Tigor and the Rio Negro when almost under the bow there appeared a triangular head and several feet of undulating body. It was a giant anaconda. I sprang for my rifle as the creature began to make its way up the bank, and hardly waiting to aim smashed a .44 soft-nosed bullet into its spine, ten feet below the wicked head. At once there was a flurry of foam, and several heavy thumps against the boat's keel, shaking us as though we had run on a snag..."

None of the reports regarding large anacondas in the Amazon count as confirmed reports.

BORARO

Not a good picture, it really doesn't fit the description. The Boraro comes to us from the northwestern part of the Amazon. The word Boraro means the Pale Ones. The creature has backwards feet, is very tall to the extent of tree size, and has pale skin, black fur, large forward-facing ears, fangs, and huge pendulous genitals. The even stranger thing about the creature is it has no joints in its knees, so if it falls down, it has trouble getting up.

The creature has two ways to kill its victims. First, it is known to urinate on them with a lethal toxin that kills the prey. Second, if it catches the victim, it crushes it, liquefying the internal organs. Then it drinks the liquid through two small holes in the head, leaving the empty skin on the ground like a deflated balloon.

The only ways to escape this horrid death are to pacify the monster with tobacco or run away backwards from the monster, which confuses the creature. I found no reported sightings, but the Tucano people very much believe the creature exists.

TAPIRE-IAUARA

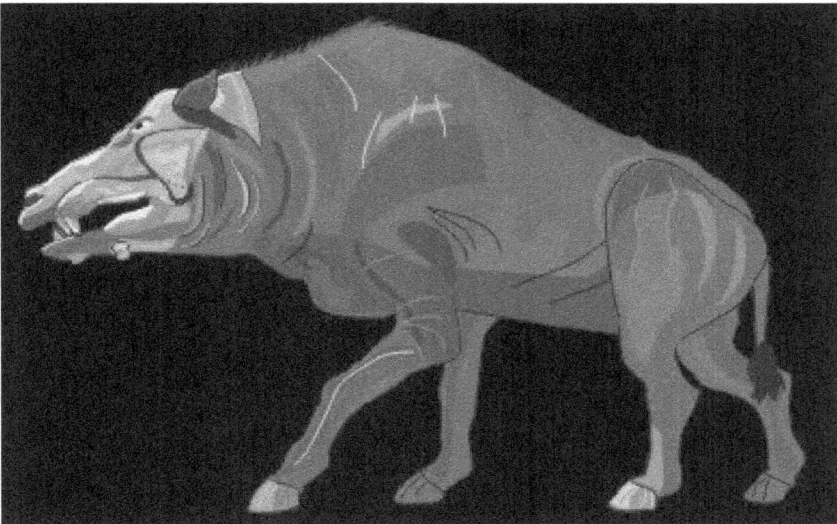

The Tapire-iauara are reported to live in remote areas in the Amazon rain forest. The creature has the appearance of a combination of a tapir and a jaguar; the creature is as large as a cow. The creature has other names like Taiacu-iara and Onca, which translates to "water jaguar" and "tapir nymph."

The reports describe red, red-gold, or even black fur with a white patch. The face is said to resemble a jaguar or cat. The ears look like large floppy cow ears. The legs look like a donkey's with hooves. It tends to be in or around bodies of water. The fur sheds water like duck feathers and exudes a strong oily smell. These creatures are excellent swimmers, and they feed mostly on fish, caiman, other aquatic prey, and may even feed on humans. They shelter in aninga groves. Often only a single one is seen, but if it feels threatened, others will come out of hiding to defend their comrade.

Hunters are said to build platforms and put a man on top to attract the creature. These creatures go up on the platform to either kill the man eating the raw fish or to take the raw fish to eat, and the creature would be shot and killed.

There is another tale that says the Tapire-iauara has the ability to steal people's souls. There are two ways the creature is said to take souls: first, when a person sees the creature, they freeze and/or faint, and it steals the soul; second, it emits a skunk-like stench that causes the soul to leave.

I found no reports of sightings, but with the beliefs in those areas, people may just be too scared to report the sightings.

MINHOCAO

The Minhocao is a giant earthworm or serpentlike creature. It has hard black scales, a piglike nose, a very definitive mouth with large sharp teeth, and two tentacles, one on each side of its mouth. The creature lives in southern Brazil, Uruguay, Nicaragua, and Bolivia. The creature is said to cause major destruction when they show up because of their size. They grow up to one hundred fifty feet long and fifteen feet wide, causing a trench that can reroute rivers. There have been no reports since the nineteenth century.

Auguste de Saint Hilaire wrote, prior to Muller's collection of eyewitness accounts:

> "The monster in question absolutely resembles these worms{earthworms}, with this difference, that it has a visible mouth; they also add, that it is black, short, and of enormous size; that it does not rise to the surface of the water, but that it causes animals to disappear by seizing them by the belly."

The creatures live in or near water; in at least one account the creature was wallowing in mud. The creature has overturned boats, grabbed livestock, pulling them underground, and even grabbed humans, taking them underground and eating them.

I found a lot of sightings, and here is the best one, in my opinion:

> According to an 1899 newspaper report, an American soldier in Cuba wrote to his family, claiming that a Cuban scout had told him about a scaly, three-foot-wide, hog-snouted burrowing animal that lived near watercourses in the jungle mountains in the east of the island. Given the lack of any other information about the Minhocao in Cuba, Chad Arment regards this story as a newspaper concoction based on Muller's reports.

Also in 1899, an Argentine government official named Florencio de Basaldua recorded claims of an amphibious monster named "Mio-ciao" living close to Santo Tome, near the Uruguay River close to the Brazilian border:

> "A great amphibian monster whose lair was in a deep pool, close to his post, he believed it to be a hippopotamus, which the Brazilians living along the shore called mio-cao, because they had seen it swim in the river and graze on its shores, assuring that it was not Danta, Anta orGran Bestia common in that area. And was not similar to any other animal that lives in those regions."

YA-TE-VEO

THE YA-TE-VEO, OR CARNIVOROUS PLANT.   476

The tree is said to live in the secluded Tepui high mountain mesa in the Guiana Highlands of South America. It grows from a singular shrub known to the native tribes as the Ya-Te-Veo, or "I See You" tree, which evolution has given a fondness for human flesh.

J. W. Buel gives us this description of this abomination in his seminal work, *Sea and Land* (1887):

> "Travelers have told us of a plant, which they assert grows in Central Africa and also in South America, that is not contented with myriad of large insects which it catches and consumes, but its voracity extends to making even humans its prey. This marvelous vegetable Minotaur is represented as having a short, thick, from the top of which radiate giant spines, narrow and flexible but of extraordinary tenaciousness, the edge of which are armed with barbs, or dagger-like teeth, instead of growing upright, or at an inclined angle from the trunk, these spines lay their outer ends upon the ground, and so gracefully are they distributed that the trunk resembles an easy couch with green drapery around it. The unfortunate traveler, ignorant of the monstrous creation which lies in his way, and curious to examine the strange plant, or to rest himself upon its inviting stalk approaches without a suspicion of his certain doom. The moment his feet are set within the circle of the horrid spines, they rise up, like gigantic serpents, and entwine themselves about him until he is drawn upon the stomp, when they speedily drive their daggers into his body and thus complete the massacre. The body is crushed until every drop of blood is squeezed out of it and becomes absorbed by the gore-loving plant, when the dry carcass is thrown out and the horrid trap is set again."

NAHUELITO

Nahuelito is a monster stalking the water of Nahuel Huapi Lake, Patagonia, Argentina. Much like the Loch Ness Monster, the creature is named after the lake it resides in. It has been described as either a giant serpent or a creature like a plesiosaur with a huge hump.

The first colonizers heard many stories from the native population about encounters with an aquatic monster.

In 1897, Dr. Clemente Onelli, director of the Buenos Aires Zoo, began to receive sporadic reports of a strange creature in the Patagonian lakes.

In 1910, George Garret worked near the Nahuel Huapi, and after navigating the lake and about to disembark, he could see a creature about four hundred meters (four hundred forty yards) away, the visible part of which was between five and seven meters (sixteen and twenty-three feet) long and protruded about two meters (six point six feet) above the water. Commenting on his experience with locals, Garret learned of similar stories told by the natives. But Garret's sighting in 1910 was only made public in 1922.

Josh Gates investigated this creature in the first season of *Destination Truth*, episode four, 2007. He used high-tech equipment in order to find evidence of the creature or disprove it. In the show he went to an island in the middle of the lake where nuclear experiments were done during World War II. But he found nothing to lead him to believe the creature was a result of nuclear testing. His investigation was not conclusive.

MALPELO MONSTER

The Malpelo monster is known by other names like Bongo or El Monstro. This is a mysterious, large, sharklike creature in the Pacific Ocean off the island Isla de Malpelo, which is two hundred eighty-five miles off the coast of Colombia. The creature is a female, about fifteen feet long, with big black eyes. The dorsal fin is located above the pectoral fins. It prefers colder water under the thermocline, below one hundred sixty feet deep.

Colombian biologist Sandra Bessudo launched an investigation in March 2001 to determine its status. During the dive at the National Malpelo Park, she came face-to-face with this gigantic unknown species of shark. She escaped but was driven to discover the shark's identity.

In 2002, she organized a risky expedition to find out more about the creature. Arriving at the spot where she had seen the shark, she discovered the area had been destroyed by a storm, and the creature was not there. She returned to the boat, and once on the boat, a band of pirates hijacked her boat and seized fourteen tons of sharks by stabbing her nets with their spears.

ACALICA

T he Acalica creatures are known to be not so ferocious; these fair-
tempered creatures are known to be weather fairies for their

power to control the weather. They are about the size of a dragonfly with four wings, are very fast, and can vary in color from red to blue, even green. They live in underground caves, and they usually avoid coming in front of the human territory.

Legend says that some humans have previously confronted the Acalicas, and they are like small and wizened men. They enjoy controlling the weather, but it is said they punish anyone who bothers them. They have also been known to mimic humans to lure people away.

I was unable to find any sightings.

UCUMAR

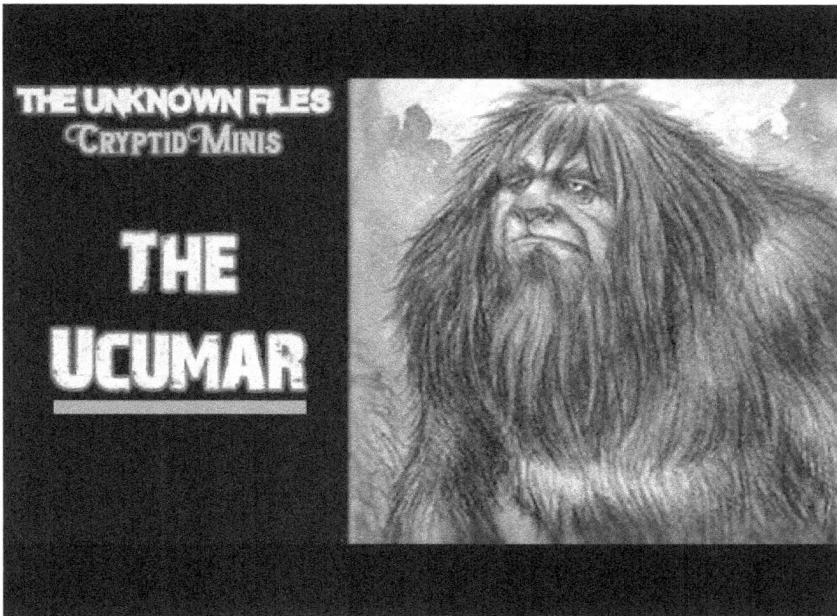

THE UNKNOWN FILES
CRYPTID MINIS

THE
UCUMAR

The Ucumar is a Bigfoot-type creature in the area around
Argentina and Chile. They describe it as five to seven feet tall,

with thick hair, small eyes, and huge arms and legs. It is reported to be a half-bear humanoid. The locals say the creature loves to eat a plant called payo, which is similar to cabbage. It also emits a sound like uhu, uhu, uhu, uhu, which Ivan T. Sanderson compared to the noises reported by Alert Ostman, who claimed to have been held captive by a family of Sasquatch in 1924.

One of the first documented sightings of the Ucumar took place in May of 1958 when a group of campers in Rengo, fifty miles from Santiago, Chile, reported that they saw what they could only describe as an ape man. Police were called out to investigate; they took reports from the witnesses, one of which was Carlos Manuel Soto, who swore that he had seen an enormous man covered in hair in the Cordilleras, one of Santiago's six provinces.

In 1956, geologist Audio L. Pich found seventeen-inch-long human-like footprints on the Argentina side of the Andes Mountains at a height of over sixteen thousand feet. The following year similar tracks were discovered in the province of La Salta, Argentina. Not long after, residents of Tolor Grande reported a nightly chorus of eerie calls emanating from the nearby Curu-Curu Mountains. The cries, which were attributed by the locals to a creature known as the Ukumar-zupai, frightened the community for some time, and according to anthropologist Pablo Latapi Ortega, traditions of these giant ape men continue to this very day in Argentina.

POMBERO

POMBERO

T his is a very interesting creature, and I hope you enjoy the story. El Pombero is not your typical monster; it is a fey or spirit. The creatures are wonders from Paraguay, Argentina, and Brazil. The Pombero can be friend or enemy depending on their mood. You can leave offerings to these elflike creatures, like tobacco, honey, or rum. The local farmers leave the offerings to receive favors such as growing crops in abundance, taking care of farmyard animals, etc. But the offering must continue for thirty days, or evil will befall them at the hands of Pombero.

There are things you should never do while in the area where the Pombero roams. Never speak his name aloud, never speak ill of him, or whistle in the dead of night, because these things anger him. He can get revenge on the person by teasing or hitting the person. The mere touch of their hairy hand can cause shingles or experiencing tremors for the rest of their life.

Pombero are described as muscular, small statured, and exceedingly ugly, with hairy hands and feet. Even though they have a horrid appearance, they are adept at seducing the fairer sex. They are believed to be able to impregnate "unappreciated" women with a mere touch or even woo them to the bedroom in a trancelike state. As a result, very ugly or hairy babies are often proclaimed to be a Pombero lovechild.

The creature is nocturnal but will occasionally venture out during the day. It sticks to rural areas, particularly forests, and sometimes seeks refuge in abandoned houses and sheds. One of his many tricks is to mimic bird sounds with incredible accuracy. Some believe he does this to protect the birds from bad local kids who hunt the birds with slingshots. The creature can also turn invisible.

I was unable to find reported sightings, but I did find videos. Also, the show *Destination Truth* did a show on it but with no real conclusion. I believe these creatures are out there; you should check out the videos online.

LA TUNDA

L a Tunda is said to have once been a human and a very abusive, controlling woman who lived in the woods with her children. When her children tried to run away from her abuse, she punished them by chopping them up and burying the body parts in her flower garden. By doing this, she imbued the flower garden with dark magic, which cursed La Tunda, turning her into a monster that seeks out disobedient children to feed her garden.

La Tunda is described as a very ugly woman with a horrid smell. She has ragged clothing, bulging brown eyes, grayish skin, looks like the dead, one foot is a molinillo (a wood whisk used to stir hot liquids), and as she walks, she grunts and complains. She looks to grab unbaptized and misbehaving children. She also takes unfaithful people to the jungle to make them her lovers or companions. She does this by shape-shifting into people they love or trust to lure them into the mountain or jungle. Once she has her victims, she feeds them shrimp and crabs that are cooked in a bewitched pot. The food hypnotizes the victim, she then shape-shifts into an attractive female or male, then she sucks out their blood, making them into her unwavering followers, rejecting their old life.

The only way to save her victims is to gather a group of people made up of godly parents, a priest, friends, and other family members. Then they all go into the area, playing drums, burning gunpowder, firing shotguns, praying prayers, and saying foul words. This makes La Tunda run away and snaps her victim out of the spell.

South America did not disappoint. Now let's see what monsters will be shown to us in the continent of Antarctica.

Part Five

ANTARCTICA

Antarctica is the southern most continent and of course the site of the south pole. It is virtually uninhabited and totally ice covered. There is a subglacial lake that flows blood red. Other than some research bases there are no towns or full-time population, only a thousand to five thousand seasonal people there. I was able to find a few monsters and here they are.

ORGANISM 46B

Organism 46B is the designation given to an aquatic beast captured by a Russian scientific team near the research outpost Vostok Station.

Organism 46B is a gigantic thirty-three-foot-long, fourteen-tentacled squid-like creature that lived in Lake Vostok, which is a subglacial lake two miles under the ice near Vostok Station. The creature could release a toxin into the water to immobilize its prey from a distance of one hundred fifty feet away. It also displayed an amazing degree of shape-shifting, its limbs were animate and aggressive even after amputation, and it showed a considerable degree of both hostility and intelligence.

The station was established in 1957 by the Soviets. In 1974 they discovered a subglacial lake under the station. After thirty years of core drilling, they finally reached the lake on the fifth of February, 2012. The only encounters happened between then and November 30, 2016. Dr. Anton Padalka claimed to have been part of the first scientific expedition to the lake. "We encountered Organism 46B on our first day. It disabled our radio—which we later learned, to our alarm, was intentional. It is able to paralyze its prey from a distance of up to one hundred fifty feet away, by releasing its venom into the water. Tragically my colleague and lifelong friend was killed this way."

Later while diving in the lake, the group was attacked; the creature released its venom into the water, which got one of the divers; the creature then grabbed him and ate him. Padalka stated, "He treaded water wearing a blissful smile as the organism approached him. We watched helplessly as it used its arms to tear off his head, then popped his remains into its mouth. It was like the diver was hypnotized telepathically."

NINGEN

In the past few years, tales have been going around Japan about the existence of arctic humanoid lifeforms living in the icy waters of Antarctica. Reportedly observed on many occasions by crew members of government-operated "whale research" ships. The creatures have been given the name Ningen, which means human.

They are white in color and about twenty to thirty meters, or sixty-six to ninety-eight feet, long. The eyewitness described them as having a humanlike shape, often with legs, arms, and even five-fingered hands. Sometimes they describe them as having fins or a mermaid-like tail or even tentacles. The creature's face has eyes and a mouth but no nose. One observer thought he saw a submarine, but as they closed in, he realized it was not a machine but something very alive; then it splashed and disappeared into the depths.

There was an article in the November 2007 issue of *MU* magazine, a Japanese publication, which was devoted to the "Antarctic Human." No other reports or sightings reported.

LARGE ANTARCTIC SEA MAMMAL

ゴジラのスケッチ

The body is covered in hair; its face has been compared to a cow or monkey with pointy ears. It is a mammal with a large saw-shaped dorsal fin. Some say it looks like Godzilla (from the movies) in size and shape. The only sighting comes from the crew of the Japanese research vessel named the *Soya* in the Lutzow-Holm Bay, Antarctica. The sighting occurred February 13, 1958. The crew reported seeing the creature moving through the water. Its existence was documented in the 1959 book *Antarctic Transport* by Mitsuji Matsumoto, captain of the *Soya*.

COLOSSAL SQUID

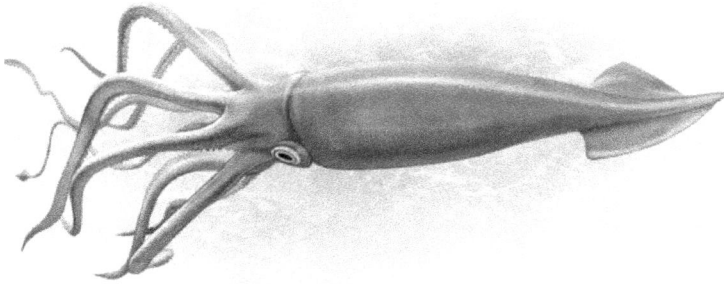

T he colossal squid is known by other names like the Antarctic or giant cranch squid and is believed to be the largest squid species. It is known from only a few specimens, and current estimates put its maximum size at twelve to fourteen meters (thirty-nine to forty-six feet) long, based on analysis of smaller and immature specimens, making it the largest known invertebrate.

Unlike the giant squid, whose arms and tentacles only have suckers lined with small teeth, the colossal squid has sharp hooks, some swiveling and others three-pointed. The body is longer and wider than the giant squid.

There have been twenty-four since they were officially discovered in 1925 in the stomach of a sperm whale.

I am sorry that there are not more monsters for this continent. People report the monsters, and with very few people passing through, not many monsters are reported.

Part Six

OCEANIA/AUSTRALIA

This continent will have more monsters than the other continents because of the number countries and islands. I want to include as many countries as possible. The main land mass is Australia, the Land Down Under. It also includes New Zealand; both places have animals that are like no others in the world. Seeing all the amazing animals that we know of in this area, I am looking forward to you seeing the ones that have not been confirmed. Open up your minds, and let's look at the creatures unconfirmed.

BUNYIP

shutterstock.com · 1707529999

The bunyip also goes by the Kianpraty, which is from the Aboriginals. They say the creature lives in the swamps, billabongs, creeks, riverbeds, and waterholes. Bunyip means devil or evil spirit.

The bunyip is described as having a doglike face, dark fur, a horse-like tail, flippers, walruslike tusk, a crocodile-like head, and a ducklike bill. It has also been described like a snake with a beard. There are many other descriptions, but all agree it is an aquatic creature.

One of the earliest accounts happened in 1818, when explorers James Meehan and Hamilton Hume discovered large bones in Lake Bathurst in New South Wales. Not knowing about the bunyip, they compared the remains to a manatee or a hippopotamus.

In July 1845, the *Geelong Advertiser* described the bunyip in detail. This was the first recorded use of the term "bunyip."

One of the legends of the bunyip tells of a man named Bunyip who broke the Rainbow Serpent's greatest law by eating his totem animal. Banished by the spirit Biami, the man became an evil spirit that lured tribesmen and their livestock into the water so he could eat them.

The last reported sighting was in 1852:

The written account is attributed to escaped convict William Buckley in his 1852 biography of thirty years living with the Wathaurong people. His 1852 account records: "in Lake Moodewarri {now Lake Modewarre} as well as in most of the other inland... is a... very extraordinary amphibious animal, which the natives call Bunyip." Buckley's account suggests he saw such a creature on several occasions. He adds: "I could never see any part except the back, which appeared to be covered with feathers of a dusty grey color. It seems to be about the size of a full-grown calf... I could never learn from any of the natives that they had seen either the head or tail." Buckley also claimed the creature was common in the Barwon River and cites an example he heard of an Aboriginal woman being killed by one. He emphasized the bunyip was believed to have supernatural powers.

YOWIE

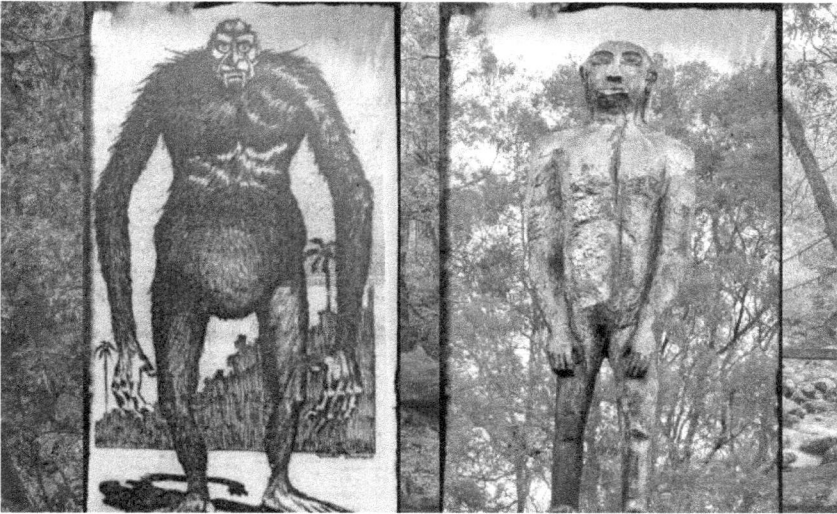

The yowie is known as the yayhoo, youree, hairy man, and yahoo. This is the Australian Bigfoot with some differences. The yowie is a fanged humanoid marsupial or great ape. The yowie is one of the most aggressive Sasquatch species and has been reported tearing off the heads of kangaroos and dogs. It has been seen attacking humans, even though it is rare.

The yowie is described to be five to nine feet tall, with a large red mouth, two large fangs, brown or reddish fur, and talonlike claws. It is believed that the yowie has the same background as the American Bigfoot.

Around twenty-six years ago, a man had a terrifying encounter with a tall, hairy creature lurking in the Queensland bush. The incident changed his life. A yowie hunter has made an alarming claim that the creature has killed innocent Australians who have unwittingly entered its territory. Dean Harrison says he has seen a yowie in the flesh; he believes some missing people may have been casualties of a yowie:

> "These things are dangerous... and I've nearly been a victim a couple of times," Mr. Harrison said. "And I know that there are other people out there that didn't get away as fortunately as I have."

Mr. Harrison said he had previously heard a yowie making an "awful noise" in his backyard when he was twenty-five, but it was two years later that he first came up close and personal with the creature in what he described as a near-death experience. He went for an evening run on a Tuesday night in 1997, but he never expected it to end with his life flashing before his eyes. He was in Ormeau, a town between Brisbane and the Gold Coast, and went for his usual run along a bush track an hour before midnight. "I heard all this crashing coming through the bush behind me and it sounded like a group of kids just trashing the place," Mr. Harrison said. The sound of snapping branches and crushing leaves started to get closer until a large figure emerged about ten meters (around thirty-three feet) behind him. "I got these unexplainable chills which are what we call the nameless dread... and like a rabbit in spotlights, basically, my whole body just locked up," he said. "I didn't know how I knew I was in danger... And I knew that if I turned around and made eye contact, things would exponentially worse."

As Mr. Harrison's flight response activated, he broke into a sprint with the seemingly aggravated creature following closely behind:

"He's yelling and roaring and he's doing some sort of almost talk over the top and on every footstep... his diaphragm in his chest would bounce," he said. "And before I knew it, he's right next to me. I thought, this is it, this is the end of my life. I'm about to die right now."

Mr. Harrison said the creature plunged towards him. He said the yowie then retreated into the bush as Mr. Harrison headed towards a streetlight.

MULDJEWANGK

The Muldjewangk is a water monster that is said to inhabit the Murray River and Lake Alexandrina. The story of the creature was used to deter children from playing near the water. Sometimes they are portrayed as evil merfolk and other times as a gargantuan monster.

The legend says a captain of a steamboat owned by European settlers saw two great hands grab the hull of his boat, so he grabbed a gun. One of the Aboriginal elders who was on board begged the captain not to hurt the creature. But the captain took aim and shot, hitting the creature, causing it to release the boat. The elder warned the captain he would suffer as a result of his actions.

Soon after the captain broke out in weeping red blisters all over his body, taking six months to die. Anyone who settled on the banks of Lake Alexandrina, the creature would pester them by wrecking their nets. The elders say the creatures are no longer around the area.

ZARATAN

The Zaratan is said to be a gigantic, small-island-size sea turtle. The shell looks like a sloped rocky mountain several hundred feet in diameter. Sailors mistakenly see its shell as a small tropical island, and in their search for fresh water and food, drop anchor and land. When night falls, the monster sinks below the surface, dragging down the ship and drowning the crew.

Other versions of the creature describe it as a giant whale, octopus, or a gigantic fish.

When Zaratan gets hungry, it is said to open its mouth wide as it exhales a sweet aroma. Fish are attracted to the pungent odor and swim in; once its mouth is full, it snaps closed like a snapping turtle.

It's one thing to look for monsters, but the game changes when the monster is an island in the ocean. No good reported sightings.

SAURIAN MONSTER

shutterstock.com · 2000703125

In October of 1886, slaughterhouse workers near Hamilton, New Zealand, arrived at work to find a sheep carcass completely eaten down to the bones. The sheep had been left high up on a hook, but whatever ate the sheep was big and strong enough to pull the sheep's body from the hook, leaving nothing but bones and footprints. The footprints were said to be some kind of lizard-like creature, giving it the name saurian. New Zealand has some reptiles but nothing the size of an alligator or crocodile.

The creature was described by one of the Maori people as being immense in size, twelve feet long, six feet wide, with large jaws, two rows of jagged teeth, and black fur or skin.

For two months, October and November, people of the Waikato region kept up a constant watch for the creature. Farm boys reported seeing it in the river, with its head poking up from the creek; indigenous Maori told settlers that they heard of the creature for some time and called it taniwha. "Stories are present among them of a very large animal, like an eel, which has come out of the water at times and chased them, even seizing their legs in its teeth." A year earlier, a Maori girl was found dead in the same river, with the flesh stripped from her arm.

TANIWHA

The taniwha is a large supernatural being that lives in deep pools
in rivers and dark caves in the sea, especially in places with
dangerous currents or deceptive breakers. They are considered highly
respected guardians of people and places, or in some traditions as
dangerous, predatory beings, which, for example, would kidnap women
to have wives.

At sea, a taniwha often appears as a whale like the southern right whale or a whale shark, or even a large shark such as the great white shark. In inland waters, it may look like a whale-size gecko or a tuatarta, having a row of spines along its back. The taniwha may even appear like a floating log.

The taniwha can have associations with tribal groups, where they become guardians of that tribe. They warn of approaching enemies, communicating the information via a priest, and sometimes save members of the tribe from drowning. There are many stories of the creatures and how they help and hinder.

Being supernatural beings, there are no real sightings of the creatures but more of a faith to believe.

MAERO

The Maero is also called Moehau, Matau, Tuuhourangi, Taongina, or Rapuwai. They are all names for the same creature, described as a "terrible creature, half-man, half-animal." The creature has been said to be very aggressive even to the point of massacre and eating anyone who strays into their domain.

Early encounters tell that the creature displays the Bigfoot trait of throwing rocks at people to get them to go away. These creatures are largely found in the Coromandel Ranges, where they were said to be responsible for a headless, partially eaten body of a prospector in the Martha Mine region in 1882. Later on, a woman's body was found; her body had been dragged from the shack while she was alone; her neck had been snapped.

Each name given to the creature also comes with a little different description. The Moehau and Maero are normal human size, unusually strong, very agile, covered with hair, and very aggressive. The Matau giants, Tuuhourangi, Taongina, and the Rapuwai are all gigantic, covered with hair, lumbering, around three meters tall (about ten feet tall), extremely strong, intelligent enough to make and use tools, and have large feet much like our Bigfoot.

In 1970, a party of campers had to abandon their campsite because a two-meter-tall (six-and-a-half-foot) man-beast assailed them, screaming and throwing rocks at the camp.

In 1972, a hunter in the Coromandel Ranges watched a naked, hairy man-beast about two meters (six and a half feet) tall work his way through the underbrush on the other side of a gully; upon reaching the place the creature had been traversing, footprints were found.

LAUTOKA DWARVES

The Lautoka dwarves were odd little hairy humanoid-type creatures that were sighted in Lautoka, Fiji. The students of the

Lautoka Methodist School reported seeing eight little hairy, bipedal creatures in the reeds near the school. The creatures were about two feet tall and covered with black hair and quickly ran into the bushes when the children approached them. When the bushes were looked at, they found a pit. The students told people, and those people told more people till almost the whole town was waiting by the hole, watching for the creatures to show back up. The creatures did not come back, at least not in that pit.

There are stories of little people or little creatures all over the world.

YARA-MA-YHA-WHO

The Yara-Ma-Yha-Who is a very odd creature, but also a very dangerous one. This little red froglike man is four feet tall with a large head and a very large mouth with no teeth, and it has suckers on the ends of its hands and feet.

The creature is said to live in the tops of fig trees. The creature does not hunt like most animals; it waits in the tops of trees, waiting for an unsuspecting traveler to rest under its tree. When the person stops under the tree, the creature drops down and uses its suckers to drain the blood from the victim. After the blood is gone, the creature unhinges its jaw like a snake and eats the body of the victim, and then it takes a nap. When it wakes from its nap, it regurgitates the victim, leaving them shorter than before. The victim's skin has a reddish tint to it that it didn't have before, and then it repeats the process time after time till the victim is transformed into a Yara-Ma-Yha-Who.

The legend says the creature is only active during the day and only targets living prey. If you "play dead" until sunset, the creature will avoid you. The story is often told to misbehaving children.

I was unable to find reported sightings.

ORANG MAWAS

The Orang Mawas is the Malaysian version of Bigfoot. It is described as being ten feet (two point four three meters) tall, bipedal, and covered in black fur. The creature has been reported to feed on fish and raid orchards. There have been many reports since the 1950s and in 1995 in Johor of large tracks with four toes.

In November 2005, a sighting occurred when three workers clearing ground for a pond saw a Mawa family of two adults and a child near the Kincin River. Afterwards, large humanoid footprints were found, including one eighteen inches (forty-six centimeters) long. A picture of a fresh footprint in tar was published in a Malaysian newspaper in January 2006.

MEGALANIA

The Megalania did exist but are considered to be an extinct species of giant monitor lizard. It is the largest lizard known to have existed, reaching a length of three point five to seven meters (eleven point five to twenty-three feet) and weighing between ninety-seven to one thousand nine hundred forty kilograms (two hundred fourteen to four thousand two hundred seventy-seven pounds). There is even a skeleton in the Melbourne Museum.

During the middle of the day, a surveyor got back to his truck, ready to go home from a long day. He saw what he believed to be a fallen tree near his truck. He got into the truck, and when he slammed the door, the "log" suddenly bolted off. It ended up being a fifteen-foot-long lizard.

In July 1979, Rex Gilroy was told that there were footprints across his newly plowed field. The field had about thirty enormous lizard tracks across it. Rain had washed away most of the tracks, but they were able to cast one print, and it was a match for the Megalania.

Megalania might not be constrained to only Australia; some sightings suggest it could be alive and well in New Guinea. A French priest in 1960s was traveling upriver with a native guide to reach his mission. During their trip, the priest saw a large lizard lying on a fallen log, sunning itself. The priest tried to get his guide to stop, but he would not. The next morning the priest returned and measured the tree, it was forty feet long, and the lizard he saw was as long as the tree.

SOLOMON ISLANDS DRAGON SNAKE

The Solomon Island dragon snake has the ability to fly and spit fire, but has a major dislike of humans. There are said to be frequent sightings of these creatures. The dragon snakes patrol the coast and mountains of the Solomon Islands. The creatures have been blamed for people going missing and people getting killed.

They describe the creature as having nocturnal behavior, seen only as a form of light or a silhouette. The body is shaped like a man, but the silhouette looks like a stingray. There is a shape at the end of the tail that resembles a diamond or triangle. They are white or black, with greenish-brown scaly skin and piercing red eyes. They have the ability to project a red glow from their bodies, which they use to draw fish in at night in the water. They are also reported to spit fire in the form of light, but it still burns upon impact. Basically, like a fireball. The size of the body light itself is around sixty feet in diameter; the wingspan might be larger or the same size as that.

The earliest depiction of the strange dragon like creature in the Solomon Islands comes from Gerard de Jode's atlas *Speculum Orbis Terrae* {Mirror of the World} from 1593. One part of the atlas depicts two flying creatures with batlike wings and a long tail with flukes. One creature has two "pelvic fins," which could be feet. The second has dermal frills. Both with long necks or snouts.

Marius Boirayon, a former RAAF engineer, bought a house in Cape Esperance. He and his friends were fishing in the night when one of his friends, Joseph, shouted about the dragon snake whilst pointing in its direction. The creature made a bright star-like light about sixty feet in diameter. After several minutes the creature submerged itself into the water. A few minutes later the creature surfaced with even stronger light. They continued to watch until its disappearance over the top of the coconut trees. The creature was seen sixty more times in seven months.

OCEANIA'S GIANTS

G iants are found in every country and in every religion. There are ancient drawings from every country as well. The definition is a human over seven feet tall, so with that definition, there are giants today playing ball and wrestling for your entertainment. It seems like anytime bones are found, governments show up, and all goes into secrecy. Here are some stories of the giants in Oceania.

On the remote atoll of Nukulaelae lived a giant called Tevalu. The giant was said to grab children playing on the beach to kill and eat them. Two brothers attacked Tevalu, throwing fishing spears into his eyes, killing the giant. A few years ago some Japanese archaeologists found what the older villagers said was the giant's grave, which was over three point five meters (eleven and a half feet) long. But they were not allowed to open the grave.

The Marshall Island has the small atoll of Lae with a legend that tells of a huge cylinder of wood that drifted on to their shore with giants inside. The villagers feared for their lives, so they attacked the weakened giants, killing them. Then one of the elders discovered that one of the giants was a princess, and the villagers regretted what they had done. Still to this day the islanders throw a piece of food in the water to beg forgiveness when they go fishing and pass by the inlet where she is buried.

Fiji has an isolated island called Rotuma north of the main islands. A three-foot-long (one-meter-long) shin bone was found while building a watch house during World War II. In the same area while searching for places to hide in case of a Japanese invasion, they found caves with giant human bones.

There are many more stories like Moso in Samoa, Moke and Teu in the Cook Islands, and Kanunu on Mangaia Island. The royal family of Tonga were said to be giants, with the king measuring two meters tall, and the bones are said to be on display.

Easter Island was reported to be populated with giants when Dutchman Jacob Roggeveen discovered the island in 1722. Bahrens, one of the members of the expedition, wrote that the natives were so tall that a man could walk upright between their legs.

There are many more stories of giants in this area. I believe more giants roam the earth than anyone knows.

ADARO

Adaro is a merperson-like creature but not like the little mermaid on Disney. These creatures are dangerous and are described as an evil, malevolent sea spirit. These creatures live and thrive in the Pacific Ocean near the Solomon Islands. These merfolk are a combination of human and fish. They are described as humanoid, shark, marlin, and most likely any sea creature. They are the size of a big human or larger. They are able to use tools and weapons, which indicates high intelligence. They are said to be very cunning, fast, and extremely cruel. There are tales of these creatures robbing ships and boats and killing the entire crew. Rumors tell of them traveling in waterspouts.

I looked at videos of merpeople and was unable to tell if they were real. They have been blamed for people disappearing at sea. If these creatures are in the Pacific Ocean, they could be all around the world, and there are reports of mermaids around the world.

GIANT TONGAN SKINK

The giant Tongan skink is an unknown lizard in the wooded forests of Tongatapu Island, Tongo. The creature is supposed to be extinct, but we know they did exist in the area. They are around eighteen inches long and one to one and a half inches wide, dull green with blackish markings.

Lannon Oldenburg saw a lizard around eighteen inches long running across the ground near Tupou College. It was dull green with black markings.

GAZEKA

The Gazeka is also known as the devil-pig and is described as a significantly larger than other Papuan New Guinea mammals, with a size of five to six feet (one point five meters) in length and three feet six inches (one meter) in height. It has been compared to pigs and also tapirs. The color is dark, possibly black, with lighter patterns vari- ably described as "pattern-like markings" or "black and white stripes." It has a long nose resembling a tapir and a tail like a horse, with cloven feet.

In 1878, Explorer Andrew Goldie claimed to have come across large, unidentifiable tracks during an expedition to the interior of British New Guinea in 1878. In size and shape, they resembled "horse's hoof with shoes on," but with "the impression of four toes." Nearby was a bodily impression showing where the animal had lain down on the sand. In his memoirs, which were published posthumously only in 2012, Goldie added that the movements of a large animal in the bush had been heard during the previous night.

In 1906, The most famous devil-pig encounter occurred during Captain Charles Monckton's expedition to Mount Albert Edward, during which he personally saw tracks, dung, and other traces of some large unknown animal, and two of his men encountered the animals themselves. Monckton's book *Last Days in New Guinea* (1922) contains an account of the incident, taken from his earlier official report in 1906:

> "Here we found the tracks of a very large, heavy, cloven-footed animal; an average spoor was measured by Mr. Money, and proved to be four inches by four and a half inches. There were others much larger; but we took an average. Excrement smaller than, but in other respects resembling that of a horse, but otherwise strange to me, was very plen- tiful. The herbage had been grazed, and in some places turned up."

On 10 May, two expedition members, an army private called Ogi, and a village constable called Oina were sent out to find a trackway but became separated, and whilst seeking Oina, Ogi came across two large piglike creatures grazing. Ogi fired on them, and the smaller one wandered off, but the larger one turned and looked at him. He saw something odd in the animal, and the carrier who was with him called it a "devil-pig." As Ogi tried to reload, the smaller one called, and the larger one walked off. Ogi himself never described the encounter in print, but Monckton recounted his experience as follows:

"After he {Ogi} had parted with Oina, the carrier with him had pointed out two enormous pigs feeding on a grass patch, He had gone within thirty yards and fired at one, but said that his hands was shaking so much with the cold that he could not hold his rifle straight. At the report of the rifle, the smaller of the two animals moved off; the larger raised its head and turned round and looked at Ogi, who perceived that there was something unusual about it. At the same time the carrier called out, 'Those are devils, not pigs!' While Ogi, partly paralyzed with cold and fright, was fumbling with a second cartridge, the animal that had at first moved off called to its mate, which at once trotted away... The description of the beast culled from a mass of statements, is that it is about five feet long, three feet six inches high, has a tail like a horse and cloven feet, black or dark skin with pattern-like markings, a long snout, grazes on grass and turns over moss with its snout, and calls with a long. Shrill note."

MENTIGI MONSTER

A modern account of mysterious remains hails from the mist-shrouded shores of Sumatra. The case was forgotten and fell through the cracks until an Indonesian marine enthusiast, Ada Emeralda, brought the story to at least minor global attention in the summer of 2000. The few details, including her report, serve as an interesting—and recent—addition to this ever-growing list.

According to Emeralda, a local newspaper report stated that on May 20, 2000, the carcass of a large unidentified animal was found on Mentigi beach, which was located approximately seventy-five miles south of Tanjung Pandan, on Belitung Island of south Sumatra. Described as being eighteen feet in length, the animal weighed three tons.

The carcass's most intriguing feature was a huge pair of tusks that measured six feet long. The carcass was compared to other carcasses found in different parts of the world. It was similar to the Egyptian "Ataka carcass," the Mexican "Tecolutla sea monster," and the lesser known Samoan "Suwarrow Island devilfish."

Emeralda's report said the stench coming from the creature's remains was so bad the natives claimed they retreated over five hundred yards but couldn't get away from it. Her report further claimed that the animal had been swimming around and playing in the water less than a mile off the Sumatran shoreline just ten days before the carcass washed up on shore.

GAJAH MINA

Gajah Mina is a cryptid creature is described as a combination of elephant and fish, and it is very well known to the Malay and Indonesian seafaring people. The name even means "fish elephant." In Balinese Hindu culture, Gajah Mina is one of the seven mythological animals (Makara). The shapes of elephant-headed fish are often painted or carved into candi (temple) as ornaments.

The description of the creature comes from the coastal village elders. The elders said that the creature is as large as a whale, has a trunk like an elephant, fur on its body, a pair of tusks, and wide ears.

On 13 January 2005, a white-furred carcass was found on Dungun beach, Riau. The carcass was found by nearby villagers, and parts of it were taken by them. The village believed the carcass was from the rare Gajah Mina. The length of the carcass was twelve point four meters (forty point six eight feet). The tail was one point eight meters (almost six feet) long; the tusks two point four meters (almost eight feet) long. The skin thickness was ten centimeters (three point nine inches). The length and width of the flippers was seventy-eight centimeters (thirty point seven inches) by forty-seven centimeters (eighteen and a half inches).

On 20 June 2010, a fisherman named Amir had his nets out and was diving to catch fish. He saw what he called a "sea elephant" was trapped in his nets. He was afraid of the creature, so he left it in the nets and left the area for three months. When he came back, only bones remained.

MANAIA

The Manaia is considered to be a mythological creature that is often carved and made into jewelry. The creature is depicted as having the head of a bird and the body of a man; it is also depicted as a bird, a serpent, a human figure in profile, and sometime as a seahorse or lizard. The Manaia is traditionally believed to be a messenger between the earthly world of mortals and the domain of the spirits, and its symbol is used as a guardian against evil. The native people use this symbol in designs of doors and windows to protect them from evil. This creature appears to be in the physical world as well as the spiritual world. There are sightings said to be related to the creature.

On August 1, 1889, Mr. Alexander Lindsay Kerr, chief officer of the union steam shipping company ship *Rotomahama*, was shocked to see what was believed to be giant conger eel, except it had two fins and was about ten feet (three meters) long. The creature also had a head more like a crocodile. The creature leaped out of the water around thirty feet (nine meters) into the air.

In April 1971, the crew of the *Kompira Maru* saw a large creature with bulging eyes about thirty kilometers (eighteen point six miles) off Lyttleton. It resembled a large crocodile with fins instead of legs.

In 1993, Earl Rigney saw what he thought was a whale in the distance. He grabbed his telescope to get a better look; that's when he went from what he thought was a whale to an up-close look at something he couldn't explain. He saw what through the telescope looked like a colossal crocodile. The creature was breaching the surface as is it was feeding, and looked to be roughly thirty feet (nine meters) long. The creature had fins not legs.

There are other sightings, but I think you can see the creature is a physical creature held in high reverence.

ABAIA

The Abaia is believed to be a gigantic eel that lives on the bottom of freshwater lakes in Fiji, the Solomon Islands, and Vanuatu. This creature guards over the fish and other creatures in the lake. The Abaia treats every fish and other creature in the lakes as if they are its children and protects them furiously against anyone who would harm or disturb them. Anyone who makes the mistake of fishing these lakes will be immediately overwhelmed by a large wave caused by the thrashing of its powerful tail.

Another legend of the Abaia states that if someone were to harm a creature living in the Abaia's home, the creature would cause a great rainstorm, flooding the land and drowning those who caused the harm.

The creature, if it's a physical creature, is most likely a large eel. No sightings to report. There are pictures of eels caught in some of the freshwater lakes.

AGTA

The Agta is a creature from the mythology of the Philippines. The creature is described as a tall, very dark-skinned humanoid that lives in the trees. They are often said to be naked and smoking a cigar. They enjoy playing practical jokes on humans and are said to lure away and kidnap women with flowers.

They warn fishermen not to go out on the water to fish and instead stay on land. If the fishermen don't heed the warning, the Agta might push over trees to stop them from going to the coast. You can scare these creatures off by carrying a bottle of mercury.

On September 18, 1963, a woman named Virginia Taglucop told folklorist Maximo Ramos that she and her sister had encountered an Agta in 1957. The two were walking along a footpath in Barrio Palanas, Masbate, where they had seen an Agta sitting under a santol tree. The Agta walked towards them for a distance of twenty-five meters before they ran away. Virginia also reported seeing an Agta smoking under a santol tree between eight p.m. and four a.m. the next morning.

KAPRE

The Kapre is another tree cryptid from the Philippines. The Kapre is described as a seven-to-nine foot-tall or two-point-one-to-two-point-seven-meter-tall, humanoid, dark-colored, long-legged, hairy creature, with strong body odor, and smokes cigarettes. The creature lives in big trees like acacias, mangos, bamboo, and banyan. They wear a belt that gives them the ability to be invisible to humans. The

Kapre is said to hold a white stone about the size of a quail egg, and if you get it from the Kapre, it will grant you a wish.

Kapre are believed to be nocturnal and omnivorous. They are not evil but can be vengeful if you cut down their tree. They are friendly overall, but they do like to play pranks. Frequently they will make travelers become disoriented and lose their way in the mountains and the woods. Sometimes they even confuse people in familiar surroundings. Reports of experiencing Kapre enchantment include rustling tree branches with little to no wind, hearing loud laughing from an unseen being, smoke from the tops of trees, seeing big red eyes, and seeing the Kapre walking in wooded areas.

I found some sightings, but most were videos, and I don't trust videos.

Now to my area, North America, with tons of real people encounters that were sent to me.

Part Seven

NORTH AMERICA

The continent of North America lays claim to the Central American area, Mexico, the United States of America, and Canada. From North America comes some of the greatest and most well-known monsters that have been thrust into the light for the world to see. The main thing you must understand when talking about monsters, here we have the unique mix of mainstream, tribal, and superstitions that have given birth to our monsters. I have twenty-plus personal encounters to share with you. Now allow me to introduce you to our first one.

MOTHMAN

We are starting with the Mothman, described as a black, ten-foot creature with wings and red eyes. It was 1966 when two gravediggers in Clendenin, West Virginia, saw a black figure fly over their heads while digging a grave in a cemetery. Little did they know, but this was the first reported sighting of the creature. Not long after that, the residents of Point Pleasant, West Virginia—a few miles west of Clendenin—claimed to have seen the creature while driving at night. Articles in newspapers at the time were reporting that the creature was also commonly seen in the TNT area near town, with some locals believing that maybe people were really seeing cranes or owls, and others wondering if the creature had been created in some sort of mutation accident involving the chemicals associated with storing the TNT left there by the government.

The most infamous sighting of Mothman was on December 15, 1967. Locals said they saw Mothman on top of—or flying over—the Silver Bridge, which was a suspension bridge over the Ohio River that connected Point Pleasant, West Virginia, to Gallipolis, Ohio. According to the Mothman legend, shortly after the creature was spotted on the bridge, the bridge collapsed, resulting in the deaths of forty-six people. An investigation into the disaster decided it was a fracture in a suspension chain. Mothman has been allegedly sighted at other disastrous events since the bridge collapse, with people claiming to have seen the creature before earthquakes, tsunamis, and even the 9/11 terrorist attack. A creature resembling the Mothman was also seen at the Chernobyl disaster.

My belief is that the Mothman is a herald of doom, sent here or sensing, I do not know. There is also a theory he is an alien.

Here is an encounter from my friend Michelle Poye and her son, Brandon Poye:

MICHELLE AND BRANDON POYE

Clay City, Indiana

It was early afternoon, and I was driving through an area that's semi-country if that makes sense, few houses far between and lots of trees, with wooded areas around. My son noticed it flying overhead and I wish I would have been able to pull over and get pictures but it happened so quickly. It flew out from the trees in front of us, glided above the tree line in our view for maybe 5 seconds as we were trying to figure out what we were seeing and then it disappeared into the trees.

It had a large wingspan (really don't have any idea on how to base size being so far away, maybe 8 ft span), the wings looked like bat wings, the body looked to be greyish in color, head reminded me and my son of a gargoyle. I noticed long skinny feet dangling as it flew away.

I know Michelle Poye and her husband, Lee Poye, they are good people, and I believe this was a true encounter.

JERSEY DEVIL

The legend of the Jersey Devil dates back to 1735 and a poor family named Leeds. The mother, Jane, was pregnant with child number thirteen. Thirteen was bad luck; the family lived in the Pine Barrens, scraping by an existence. She complained to family and friends that "the Devil can have this one," and he did.

The story says when the baby was born, it was a grotesque monster.

The "baby" grew to twenty feet long with a reptilian body, a horse's head, giant bat wings, and a long forked tail. It destroyed the room before disappearing up the chimney. The creature made the Pine Barrens its home and was dubbed the Jersey Devil. The story spread rapidly; even grown men wouldn't venture out at night. The creature was said to carry off large dogs, geese, cats, small livestock, and even small children. The Jersey Devil is said to have supernatural powers. The Devil can dry up milk cows by breathing on them, and kill off fish from streams, threatening the regional livelihood.

In 1740, the residents of the Pine Barrens begged a local minister to exorcise away the creature for one hundred years, but it didn't work. In 1800, a naval hero named Commodore Stephen Decatur visited the Hanover Iron Works to test the plant's cannonballs. He noticed a strange, winged creature overhead. He supposedly took aim and fired. They say he hit the creature with no effect. I find that very unbelievable; shooting at something flying with a cannon is nearly impossible.

The second sighting was reported by a reliable witness, Joseph Bonaparte, the former king of Spain and the brother of Napoleon. Joseph leased a country house near Bordertown from 1816 to 1839. He reported seeing the Jersey Devil while hunting game one day in the Pine Barrens.

In 1840, a minister warned that the Devil had returned. Sheep were snatched from their pens, and children who were outside after sunset disappeared. The people were so scared they locked their doors and hung lanterns out at night across south Jersey. The stories continued to be told, and the lore of the Devil was recalled throughout the 1800s, although actual sightings of the creature were few. Then, in 1909, the Jersey Devil returned, and thousands of people spotted the monster or saw his footprints. It became so bad that schools closed, and people refused to go outside.

A police officer named James Sackville spotted the creature while walking his beat one night. He was passing along a dark alley when a winged creature hopped into the street and let out a horrific scream. Sackville fired his revolver at the beast, but it spread its wings and vanished into the air.

In 1909, E. W. Minster, the postmaster of Bristol, Pennsylvania, heard an eerie almost supernatural sound and saw a large creature flying diagonally, emitting a glow. The creature let out a noise that was a combination of a squawk and a whistle, then disappeared into the darkness.

On January 19, 1909, Mr. and Mrs. Nelson Evans were awakened by the sound of something on the roof of their shed. They opened the front door and shined light at their shed and saw what they described as a three-and-a-half-foot-high creature, with a face like a collie, and a head like a horse. It had a long neck, wings about two feet wide, and the back legs were like those of a crane with horse hoofs. One afternoon that same week, Mrs. J. H. White was taking clothes off the clothesline when she noticed a strange creature huddled in the corner of her yard. She screamed, then fainted, and her husband rushed out of the house to find his wife on the ground, with the Devil close by, "spurting flames." He chased it off with a stick.

A short time later, the Devil attacked a dog belonging to Mrs. Mary Sorbinski in South Camden. She heard her dog cry out after she let it out. She dashed outside with her broom in hand to find the Devil with her dog. She attacked the Devil with her broom and grabbed her dog; the Devil had torn a chunk of meat out of her dog, then flew away. She took her dog to the animal hospital and called the police. She came home to find over a hundred people around her house, watching the Devil flying around her house. When the cops showed up, one of them emptied his revolver at the Devil. It screamed and disappeared into the night. The Philadelphia Zoo offered a $10,000 reward for the capture of the Devil, but there were no takers. Hoofprints were found, but the Devil had vanished again.

In 1927, a cab driver was changing a tire one night. As soon as he had finished and lowered the cab back to the ground, the car began to shake violently; he looked up to find a gigantic, winged creature hitting his car. He jumped into the car and sped off.

In 1930, berry pickers at Leeds Point and Mays Landing got the surprise of their life when they saw the Devil crashing through the fields, eating the berries.

In 1951, a group of kids were cornered by the Devil at the Duport Clubhouse in Gibbstown. Something scared the creature, and it flew off without hurting anyone. Dozens of witnesses saw it before it vanished in the sky. There are still sightings today, but some believe it to be a hoax.

What do you believe?

WAMPUS CAT

The wampus cat is described as a feline humanoid, with black fur, glowing yellow eyes, a long tail, and oversize fangs. The creature is very fast and agile. It is said to live in the Appalachian Mountains.

The wampus cat is said to have been a beautiful Indian woman.

Her husband and the other warriors of her tribe were always going on hunting trips to feed the tribe, but the women had to stay home. She secretly followed her husband one day when he went hunting with the other men. She hid behind a rock, clutching the hide of a mountain lion around her, and spied on the men as they began the ritual.

According to the rule of the tribe, it was forbidden for a woman to hear or see the sacred ritual. So when the Indian woman was discovered, the medicine man punished her by binding her into the mountain lion skin she wore and then transforming her into a terrible monster—half woman and half mountain lion, black as her twisted soul. She was cursed and doomed to roam the hills, howling desolately because she desires to return to her normal body.

A man was hunting one night with his dogs when they both whimpered and ran off the path. At that moment, the woods were overpowered with a horrible smell like that of a wet animal that had fallen into a bog after it messed with a skunk. Then some creature howled on the path behind him, and he whirled around, dropping his rifle. His heart pounding out of his chest with fear, he found himself staring into the big, glowing yellow eyes of the wampus cat. The creature had huge fangs dripping with saliva and blood. It looked kind of like a mountain lion, but it was walking upright like a man.

With a scream of terror, the man leapt backwards and ran as fast as he could through the woods, the wampus cat on his heels. He fled to the home of a friend who lived nearby, and burst through the front door only a breath ahead of the creature. His friend slammed the door in the face of the wampus cat. Instantly, it started shuddering under the weight of the attacking monster. The man's friend grabbed his Bible and started reading aloud from Psalms. Upon hearing the holy words, the wampus cat howled in frustration and then slowly abandoned its attack and went back into the woods.

The man spent the rest of the night at his friend's place. When he went home at daybreak, he found his dogs huddled in the barn, shaken but still alive. The man never hunted after dark again.

WENDIGO

The wendigo is a horrifying creature of the Algonquian culture, who devours human flesh to survive a harsh winter.

One story says the first-ever wendigo was a lost hunter. During a brutally cold winter, the man's intense hunger drove him to cannibalism. After feasting on another human's flesh, he transformed into a crazed man-beast, roaming the forest in search of more people to eat.

In another version of the story, the first wendigo is said to have been a warrior who made a deal with the Devil. In order to save his tribe, he gave up his soul and was transformed into a wendigo.

When peace ensued, there was no need for such a fearsome creature, and the warrior was banished from his tribe and forced to live as an outcast.

The Algonquians are some of the most extensive and numerous of the Native American groups in the North America, and they once lived along the Atlantic Coast and the Great Lakes Region. Wendigo-like creatures are also found in the legends of other Native American tribes, including the neighbors of the Algonquians, the Iroquois. Among these people, a creature known as the Stone Coat bears some similarities to the wendigo.

One translation of the word "wendigo" means "the evil spirit that devours mankind." Another translation, said to be made by a German explorer around 1860, equates the word "wendigo" with "cannibal." Wendigo are said to have an insatiable hunger for human flesh—no matter how much flesh they eat, they remain hungry.

This hunger is reflected in their appearance, as extremely thin. Despite their gaunt physiques, wendigo are described by some as giants, measuring at about fourteen point eight to fifteen feet in height. Though there are slight variations as to the physical description of this creature amongst the different Algonquian peoples, it is generally agreed that wendigo have glowing eyes, long yellowed fangs, long tongues, and they are said to have sallow and yellowish skin, though others say that they are matted with hair or have decaying skin.

According to ethnohistorian Nathan Carlson, it's also been said that the wendigo has large, sharp claws and massive eyes like an owl. However, some other people simply describe the wendigo as a skeleton-like figure with ash-toned skin.

Different versions of the wendigo say different things about his speed and agility and claim he is unusually fast and can endure walking for long periods of time, even in harsh winter conditions. Others say he walks in a more haggard manner, as if he is falling apart. But speed wouldn't be a necessary skill for a monster of this nature. Once it has infiltrated human minds, he can turn them into wendigo as well, instilling the same lust for human flesh that he himself has.

The most famous case is that of Swift Runner, a Native American man who murdered and ate his whole family during the winter of 1879. Swift Runner claimed to be possessed by a "wendigo spirit" at the time of the murders. His claims fell on deaf ears, and he was hanged for his crime.

Some believe that the human personality continues to reside within the wendigo, specifically where its heart should be. This person is frozen, and the only way to kill a wendigo is to kill the human within it as well.

The Algonquian tribes blamed many unsolved disappearances of people on wendigo attacks. At the beginning of the twentieth century, an eighty-seven-year-old by the name of Jack Fiddler was tried for the murder of a woman.

He pleaded guilty to the crime; he defended himself by saying that the woman was on the verge of transforming into a wendigo, as she was being possessed by the evil spirit. Therefore, she had to be killed before she murdered other members of the tribe. In addition to this woman, Fiddler claimed to have slain at least thirteen other wendigo during his lifetime.

Believers say that the wendigo are still out there in the woods. And underneath that terrifying, flesh-eating demon, there might still be a human man who was once just a hungry hunter.

DOGMAN

The dogman is described as bipedal, seven feet tall, with blue or amber eyes, and is considered to be half man, half wolf. They're fur covered with the same coloring as a wolf, although black fur seems to be the most reported color of fur. Most people seem to think that the dogman is a new cryptid, but that's not exactly true. The first report was in 1887 in Wexford County, Michigan, when two lumberjacks saw a creature that they described as having a man's body and a dog's head. I'm sure some people believe that a dogman and a werewolf are the same creature, but I would disagree. I believe the dogman is a species, and a werewolf is a cursed human.

Human and canine hybrids go as far back as ancient Egypt in 2055 BC with Anubis. And many others after that. The Romans had a god that was a human-dog hybrid call Hermanubis in AD 100. The human-dog hybrids are talked about in almost every continent throughout history. Pliny the Elder wrote his account of ancient knowledge about the natural world. He created an encyclopedic book called *Natural History* around AD 50. In the book he talked about a tribe of human-dog hybrids living in the mountains of India:

"The heads of dogs, and cloth themselves with the skins of wild beast. Instead of speaking they bark; and, furnished with claws, they live by hunting and catching birds."

There are even depictions of Saint Christopher as being a human-dog hybrid. It seems these creatures have been seen everywhere around the world and are almost as old as humans themselves. I was lucky enough to have a good guy send me his encounter with these creatures.

THE ENCOUNTER COME TO US FROM STEVEN GLENN:

Hello all I am Steven. I have been researching Dogman for the last 20 years and have had two encounters. Both were in my back yard. I live in a National Forest in Alabama, and I was younger at the time. The first I was alone and just finished watching a movie. I heard rustling outside my back window, I walked over and looked out. The motion light came on and I saw what I thought was a large dog. It was blackish charcoal colored. I made a sound, and it noticed I was there and stood up on its hind legs to peer into the window. The window was 7 foot off the ground. I left the room and went to bed. It made some more noise then went on. A couple days later I was walking around the back of my house which backs up into the woods. It was dusk. I was walking around to get wood when I heard a growl. The growled continued and I saw

MONSTERS OF THE WORLD

the amberish eyes reflecting what was left of the sun light. It was postering like many other predators do. It was letting me know I was on its territory. I kept it in my eye shot as I backed away slowly. I did not run as being around other predators, this will initiate the instinct to chase, and I walked backwards until I reached my house and then ran in. I grabbed a shotgun just in case, but I knew of it wanted to attack me it would have. These encounters sent me on the last 20 years journey.

BOAR TUSK MONSTER

The boar tusk monster is believed to be a very large, shaggy, wild boar, with large tusks. It has been compared to the Erymanthian boar. Killing the Erymanthian boar was one of the twelve labors of Hercules. The creature was said to be enormous, with giant tusks and skin that was so strong that a spear could not penetrate it.

HERE IS AN ENCOUNTER WITH THIS CREATURE THAT WAS SENT TO ME FROM RICKY CRUMBLEY:

Just a couple miles north of Coners Georgia, on the banks of the Yellow River, sits a small cotton mill village with a population of around 600 people. Milstead Georgia was founded in 1902. Along the eastern edge of the village runs a small spring fed branch (creek) called Boar Tusk Branch. This small stream starts near main street in olde town Conyers and gently strolls for just a couple of miles before joining the Yellow River at a junction known as "Big Rock." From the early 1900's through at least the 1980's the creek traveled entirely through a heavily wooded corridor. Of course, today that corridor has been all but wiped out with roads, subdivisions, and businesses. This is the layout of the area which the monster once roamed.

The Boat Tusk Monster was a totally nocturnal creature. As far as I know it was never seen in the light of day. But as dusk fell over the village the monster would lurk in the darkness watching and waiting for its next meal. Most of the terrifying encounters would happen in the wooded corridor between "Mary Jane's spring" and "the Big Rock." The Monster seemed to hate fire, or maybe it was just light in general. Because campfires or lanterns were usually the catalyst for its aggressive behavior. I will tell of just a couple interactions. But over the years there were hundreds of stories.

First encounter: A group of 4 young boys, from the age of 14 to 17, decided that they had heard enough of the tales of "The Monster." So, they planned a campout to show that they were not afraid of the Boar Tusk Monster. They planned everything out. On Saturday morning the four guys went to an area about halfway from the spring to the rock. One of the youngsters brought his coonhound along. They cleared out a camping spot within a few yards of the creek. They gathered plenty of firewood. They had a wonderful day in preparation for their adventure. As darkness started to descend on the creek bottom, the guys built a small campfire. They roasted hot dogs over the fire for dinner, and toasted marshmallows for dessert. This was a typical campout. Everyone was having a great time. That was until the coon hound started snarling into the darkness. He was locked onto a spot in the darkness. The hound hunkered down to his belly and backed slowly into the tent. The guys got really apprehensive. But didn't panic. Each guy had brought a flashlight with them. So, they decided to all turn their lights on and in that direction at the same time. When they did, their lights hit a creature the was dark black with long fur(hair) and was huge. This thing was several times larger than their hound. It was just outside the ring of fire light. And backed off a bit from the flashlights. But it didn't leave. The guys could hear heavy steps in the leaves as it made a semi-circle around them. But it stayed out of their lights. They couldn't see it anymore. The boys all hurriedly put more and more wood on the campfire. They wanted more light. They were terrified. The dog started whimpering and came slinking up to his owner. The hound could keep up with where the creature was better than the boys. But none of them could keep track with it. It seemed to only make noise when it wanted to. And could move completely silent when it wanted to. The monster seemed to be taunting them. Any time the firelight would start to dim, they would hear the heavy footsteps. So, the boys would pile on more wood. But they knew they didn't have enough wood to keep a high fire all night. They didn't know what to do. Suddenly the hound took off running and squalling. He had taken all he could stand and was making a break for home. The boys followed too. Without a word they all busted out for home following the dog. They all made it home safely. But not one of those four boys, or the dog, ever went back into those woods. Their Dad's went back for the tent and other camping equipment the next morning. The tent was shredded to bits. The tent poles were snapped. And all of the food was gone.

This other story is not a child's story. This gentleman was 42 years old when this encounter happened. This man was fishing at "The Big Rock." He had been fishing for catfish in the Yellow River at the mouth of Boar Tusk Branch. He was fishing alone one afternoon. He had fished this spot his whole life. Never had any thoughts of The Boar Tusk Monster. He like most people had heard all of the stories and marked them up as folklore. But this day changed all of that. The fisherman was having a great day of fishing. He had caught a stringer full of catfish. It was starting to get dusky dark. Since he had no lantern or flashlight, he decided it was time to head home. He had a lot of fish to clean. So, he gathered up his fishing gear and his stringer full of catfish. As he headed up the well-used trail back towards the road, he got an uneasy feeling. He hadn't heard anything or seen anything. Something just didn't feel right. So, he kept trying to look over his shoulder without making it obvious. But he didn't see anything. So, he tried to shrug it off. The trail he was walking on was winding down beside the Boar Tusk Branch. The brush was very thick on each side of the trail. It was virtually impenetrable. As he reached a small clearing in the trail, he heard a cracking rustling sound off to his right coming out of that super thick tangle. Before he could even register the thought, He was hit with such force that it knocked him into the creek. He said that all he could see was black hair, claws, and teeth. This creature submerged him in the shallow creek. As quickly as it began it was over. The Monster grabbed the stringer of catfish in his mouth and was gone. The astonished man was bewildered and injured. He scrambled out of the creek and raced up the trail and all the way home. Amazingly he was not bitten. But he was severely scratched and had bruised ribs from the impact of the hit. Fellow has not been fishing since that day.

CIPACTLI

The Cipactli comes to us from Aztec mythology. Cipactli was a primeval sea monster, part crocodile, part fish, and part toad or frog. They are always hungry, and every joint has a mouth. The deity Tezcatlipoca sacrificed a foot when he used it as bait to draw the creature nearer. He and Quetzalcoatl created the world from its body. The cryptid creature is said to be a giant crocodile that lives in the rivers of Central America and southern Mexico. They eat fish, red meat, chickens, and birds. Disappearances of people and farm animals have been attributed to this creature.

I was unable to find any sightings or encounters.

CHUPACABRA

The chupacabra is known for attacking livestock and pets. The name chupacabra means "goatsucker," and there are two very different versions of how it looks.

In Puerto Rico, the creature is a reptilian, walking on two legs, which was the creature in the first reported sighting. There is also a canine version, which is reported in Central America, Mexico, and the United States. There have been more than two thousand sightings of both types.

The reptilian version has leathery or scaly greenish-gray skin, sharp spines or quills running down its back and, in some reports, leathery wings. It stands approximately three to four feet tall and hops in a similar fashion as a kangaroo. The creature is said to be able to hop twenty feet. This variety is said to have a dog or panther-like nose and face, a forked tongue, and large fangs. It hisses and screeches when alarmed; it also emits a sulfuric smell. The eyes glow an unusual red that causes nausea when seen by witnesses.

The dog-like version is described as a breed of wild dog, hairless, spinal ridge, pronounced eye socket, fangs, claws, and blueish-gray skin.

The first known attack was in March of 1995 in Puerto Rico. Eight sheep were discovered dead, each completely drained of blood. Each one had three strange puncture wounds in the chest. The woman who first sighted the monster, Madelyne Tolentino, had an eyewitness description that was the basis for the most famous drawing of the chupacabra in the world. In Canovanas, about thirty citizens claimed to have seen the creature, swearing that it had swooped down from the sky and leapt over the treetops. It wasn't until November 19, 1995, that a detailed description of the creature came from an eyewitness. On that autumn night in Puerto Rico the creature struck again. Farmers woke to a horrid scene. Dozens of turkeys, rabbits, goats, cats, dogs, horses, and cows were dead with no explainable cause. Just mysterious markings left by the blood-drinking creatures.

In August of 2008 in DeWitt County, Texas, the footage from the video of two police officers shows a canine-like animal running on the side of the road. The animal in the video appears to be furless with a long snout and pointed ears.

HUAY CHIVO

The stories of the Huay Chivo can be heard in Mexico's Yucatan, Campeche, and Quintana Roo regions, the northern region of Guatemala, and the jungle area of Belize. For the last hundred years or more, the Huay Chivo has been depicted as a half man, half goat. The

Huay Chivo is a brujo that transforms itself at will and only during the night. The creature is bipedal and has glowing red eyes, thick black fur, horse- or goatlike legs, the torso of a human, and the head of a goat. It is said to be between four and six feet tall.

The creature has been blamed for the deaths of cattle, goats, and chickens. It is a creature of the night. If the creature is near you, there will be a foul smell in the air, and you will feel a wave of cold air. If you make the mistake of seeing the Huay Chivo, look away because looking in the creature's glowing red eyes will cause a fever, and you will start feeling sick.

A Yucatan farmer in a temporary work program in Quebec, Canada, was interviewed in a 2012. The man retells what happened to his brother when he saw the Huay Chivo:

"You see if things at night over there, creatures, they pass by, there are creatures' half-animal and half-human, Huay Chivos, Huay Peks or Huay Mis, and you cannot kill them. My grandfather told me once there was three men, they fired their rifles at it, but it just continued running, then it turned around, paused, and looked at each one. The day after that, one of them passed away, and within this week, so did the other two. You know, when you see these things, you should wait to talk about them. At least because the malo aire will be better by then.

"They say when the huay chivo talks, it bleeds from the mouth, it has a glowing red eyes and if you look straight into its eyes, you can be frozen from fear. My brother was talking when he saw the huay chivo pass by, suddenly, he could no longer talk, he froze and two hours later he could move. They say you must have a cross, put holy water on it and then leave it on your door, the huay chivo will leave you alone after that. They say they are everywhere, where my grandparents are (Yucatan) and my uncle says if you don't do a novena for someone who has passed, they will become a huay chivo."

DEVIL MONKEY

Devil monkeys have a reputation of being aggressive, malicious, feral, and very loud. They stay in groups and are never alone. They use scouts like regular monkeys do. There is no real description because they resemble baboons and other primates. These monkeys are believed to be escaped monkeys from zoos and private owners. They are known to make horrible screaming sounds and have wild behavior, attacking people on sight and causing widespread panic. The devil monkeys do not avoid people. They have traits such as glowing red eyes, abnormal size, incredible strength, amazing speed, and even ghostly traits like causing mist or shadows to manifest wherever they go.

In the 1970s, more reports of devil monkeys came to pass, with some claiming the creatures were killing and mutilating livestock. In every account the beast had strange features like bushy tails, long snouts, and abnormal aggression, all of which made cryptozoologist Loren Coleman convinced that the devil monkeys were very real.

In 1996, a woman named Barbara Mullins was driving along Highway 12 in Louisiana when she noticed a large dead animal on the side of the road that just didn't look right. She pulled her car over and walked up to the dead animal, to get a big shock. She found a creature that looked like a baboon, not what she expected. It had shaggy thick hair, pointy ears, and apelike arms and legs, and was the size of a large dog.

LA LECHUZA

T here is a story that has been heard all over Mexico and Texas. La
Lechuza is a giant owl that is a white or black shape-shifting

witch that is seven feet tall and has a fifteen-foot wingspan. Although it is an owl, it has the face of an old woman. It was reported around Chihuahua, Coahuila, Durango, Nuevo Leon, and Tamaulipas and around the Rio Grande Valley in Texas and California.

According to most variations of the legend, the Lechuza was once a woman who was wronged and now seeks revenge. Sometimes villagers killed her child; other times the child was killed by a drunk (she is known to attack drunkards). Some other versions of the legend tell that the witch herself was killed by locals and came back to seek revenge. Which version you hear depends on where you are located. The creature has the ability to mimic the cry of a baby or whistles. The creature uses it to lure you outside, where it grabs you up to make you its meal. It has even been said that the creature's cry is an omen of death. The creature is large enough to carry a grown adult away to be its meal. It is said to be able to bring storms and cannot be killed or hurt by guns. The creature also preys on human emotion, often appearing during domestic disputes, where it waits to ambush its next victim.

According to legend, salt can protect against it; add salt on your windows and doorways at night for protection. If you see the creature, you should cuss her out to drive it away, But be careful, it is said to make the creature mad. Tying a rope of seven knots and hanging it on your door will also protect you, since it is a sign of acknowledgment and respect towards the creature. Some say praying can also save you, specifically the Magnifica (Magnificat), a prayer from the gospel of St. Luke, but it must be recited in Spanish and backwards.

I have an encounter I received from Maria Elena Hernandez.

LA LECHUZA

By: Maria Elena Hernandez

I am Mexican American/Chicana, third generation U.S. born; of Mexican descent from my great-grandparents. In our Mexican folklore, there is a story about the "Lechuza"; It is allegedly a witch who can turn herself into a bird, usually an owl or a black bird; and it can be sent to you by someone who wishes to cause you harm; but we were told that if you prayed certain prayers backwards, you could make it fall out of the sky and it would convert back into its human form. In the 1960's when I was a teenager, my grandma and all my aunts, and one uncle who never married and lived with Grandma, and a couple of adult cousins, would all sit outside on my grandma's porch in McAllen, Texas, and stay up real late at night, and my relatives would tell scary stories about the creature they called "La Lechuza." My Grandma and aunts (I called them my "Tias" and my "Tio" in Spanish and my grandma was my "Abuelita") would tell stories of how a witch could turn herself into a bird at night when she made a deal with the devil. My Tias said that some people who wanted to hurt other people would pay the witch to turn into a Lechuza and scare or harm other people. Sometimes the bird she turned into would look like an owl, or sometimes just a big, black bird. The Lechuza would allegedly fly around and do evil spells on people, or sometimes she would somehow get into their houses at night and suck their blood, and she especially liked to suck the blood of babies. In the mornings some of the women would wake up with purple bruises all over their bodies, and sometimes if they had a baby in the house the baby would wake up with purple welts and bruises all over its little body. And they would say "La Lechuza got in last night!" I would always just laugh and laugh at them because I considered myself educated, after all I was in high school and made good grades and spoke English better than they did, they mostly spoke Spanish, and I had an excellent English vocabulary! I told them I had classes in Science and Biology in high school and I had never read about any animal called La Lechuza in any of my science or biology books. So, I thought I knew everything! I would just tell them they were all loco—crazy, that there were no Lechuzas and that they were just fake stories from Mexico to scare people and kids. I felt so much smarter than all my relatives and was very smug at the time. I would listen to their stories and laugh; and they would just stare at me shaking their heads. Well, one night when we were all sitting outside on my grandma's porch, we heard my Uncle Jose coming down the alley (my grandma's house was in an alley); My Grandma said, "Oh no, here comes Jose, and he is drunk!" My Tio Jose, may he rest in peace, was a very good man, but he used to drink in the local Cantinas every weekend and would sometimes come to my grandma's house drunk after the bars closed at 2am to sleep it off. We could hear him cursing and yelling as he was coming down the alley to Abuelita's house, and as he got closer, we could see that for some reason he was flapping his hat in the air above his *head as he walked and cursing at the sky. As he got to our porch, we all suddenly heard this horrible screeching/screaming, whistling sound above us in the air, it was like a mix between a bird sound and a woman screaming or cat screeching; the most horrible sound I had ever heard! I felt an evil sensation course through my body, like electricity, and I felt immediate extreme fear. I saw that all around me my grandma, my Tias and my Tio and my cousins all got down on their knees and began to make the sound of the Cross and pray. I was in shock for a few seconds; then I heard that horrible sound again; this time it seemed to be right above the roof of my Grandma's house—it started as a whistle and ended as a woman's scream—my blood curdled and my knees shook as I fell to the floor and began praying too; all around me my Grandma, all my aunts, my adult cousins, and my uncle were down on their knees and praying in what sounded like some weird language—then I realized they were praying the Our Father and the Hail Mary backwards! I was so scared and felt such an evil presence! The Lechuza then flew directly over the house once again screaming and whistling! At this point my Tio Jose walked into the house and said: "That damn Lechuza! She has been following ever since I got out of the Cantina! She was trying to flap at my head with one of her wings!" Then I realized that was why he had been waving his hat in the air—he had been trying to keep it away from his head! Tio Jose said he knew who sent her; he said it was one of the Cantina women whom he apparently had broken up with and who had told him she was going to curse him so no other woman would want him! My Grandma told him he was lucky that the Lechuza did not flap him on the head with one of her wings, or it would have driven him insane! Well, needless to say, that night I became a believer. No, it was not an owl, it was not an eagle or a crow, or a cat, or any other natural animal. The sound it made as it flew over my grandma's house was part human, part animal, part bird, I don't know— but I knew for certain that it was not any creature in any of my science and biology books! I told my grandma, my Tios and Tias that I was sorry I had made fun of them, and that now I believed. They just looked at me and said, "Well, now you know!" I stopped going to my grandma's house at night for a while, and when I did, I left early! Many years later I heard a Lechuza again, but it was just flying by as I was walking at night—whistling and screaming; but I did not feel she was directed towards me; however, I felt the same fear as the first time I heard one and I made the sign of the Cross as it flew above me. I have never heard one again after that. This was happened in 1966. I am now 73 years old, and much wiser; when my grandchildren make fun of my stories, I just tell them that I hope they never hear what I heard and experienced at my Abuelita's house.*

PUKWUDGIE

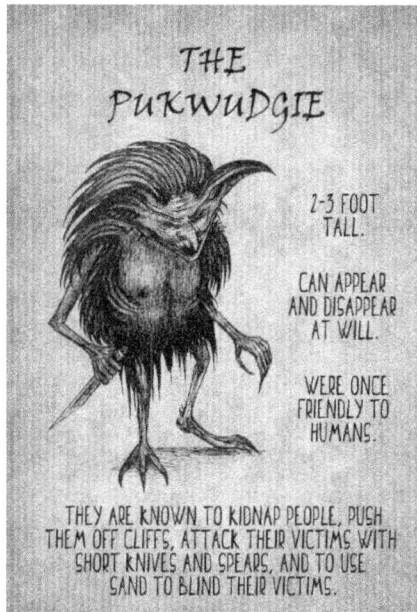

THE PUKWUDGIE

2-3 FOOT TALL.

CAN APPEAR AND DISAPPEAR AT WILL.

WERE ONCE FRIENDLY TO HUMANS.

THEY ARE KNOWN TO KIDNAP PEOPLE, PUSH THEM OFF CLIFFS, ATTACK THEIR VICTIMS WITH SHORT KNIVES AND SPEARS, AND TO USE SAND TO BLIND THEIR VICTIMS.

A Pukwudgie, also spelled Puk-Wudjie, is humanlike and said to be two-to-three-feet-tall (sixty-one to ninety-one centimeters).

According to legend, Pukwudgies can appear and disappear at will and shape-shift. The most common form is a creature that looks like a porcupine from the back and a half-troll, half-human from the front and walks upright and lures people to their deaths. They use magic, launch poison arrows, and create fire.

Native Americans believed that Pukwudgies were once friendly to humans, but then turned against people and should be left alone. According to lore, a person who annoys a Pukwudgie would be a victim of nasty tricks by the creature, or subject to being followed by the Pukwudgie, who would cause trouble for them. They are known to kidnap people, push people off cliffs, attack their victims with short knives and spears, and to use sand to blind their victims.

Pukwudgies are said to be the enemies of culture heroes Maushop and Granny Squannit. One story from Wampanoag folklore explains that they began causing mischief and tormenting the tribe out of jealousy of the devotion and affection the tribe had for Maushop, who eventually exiled them to different parts of North America. The Pukwudgies have since been hostile to humans and took revenge by killing Maushop's five sons. Some variations even suggest that they killed Maushop himself.

HERE IS AN ENCOUNTER FROM WILLIAM ROOCK:

Okay. sorry if it's been a bit. but we've got these things. 3 to 4 foot tall. That just run through the yard. they are straw/hay colored. like 4 months ago. I was playing the baby in the corner. (At this time, I've only seen these things like twice. didn't think anything of it) but the wife goes. "Did you see that" and she described it. as a short hay colored bipedal thing running across the yard. super-fast by the way. When we get up to look, they're gone.

My sisters dog died so I went to help my nephew bury her. and their woods and our woods connect. like... she's on the complete other side of the wooded area. and I was telling my nephew about the creatures. And he goes... "oh! Like what my mother's been seeing" and I was like "what!?" But she sees them when she lets the other dogs out. like 3 times at this point. shed open the door. and they would take off...

Like 3 weeks ago now. I was sitting on the couch. Wife was about to come home from work. and our dog goes ballistic. woke the baby. so, I jump up. and this time it wasn't running. it was walking. I saw it go behind the car. slowly. (Short hay colored bipedal thing) so. I grab a gun. and we stand on the porch waiting for it to come out. but 5 minutes. and nothing. But the dog refused to take her eyes off the area where we saw it for like 30 minutes until wife came home. (Really odd behavior for her, the dog not the wife)

Well. It's probably 3 to 4 foot tall. thin. Straw colored. Never seen a face. Quick. Never heard them.

A native American guy I work with says he seen them in Oklahoma, or something similar... but he says never in Missouri.

Wife had a theory it's something with her garden. we put up a fairly large green house about the time we started seeing these things...

RAVEN MOCKER

The Raven Mocker, or Kalona Ayeliski, is a creature like no other. It is the grim reaper of the Cherokee. The Raven Mocker is a shape-shifting creature that can appear as an old man, old woman, a wolf, Bigfoot, or even a raven. It is the most feared of the witches or wizards in Cherokee mythology. It comes to take the life of the sick, the old, or the dying. Once this evil spirit shows up, all other evil spirits run away. Upon arriving, you can hear what sounds like a diving raven, and without leaving a mark, it takes the heart of the person, then eats it. The creature extends its life by eating the hearts of its victims. The Raven Mocker is invisible to everyone except a medicine man.

I found references that stated a strong medicine man can do rituals to stop the Raven Mocker, and this ritual will kill it within seven days. Once the Raven Mocker is dead, other witches will find the body by digging it up; then they will abuse it because of fear and hatred.

The following is told on the reservation as an actual happening. A young man had been out on a hunting trip and was on his way home when night came on while he was still a long distance from the settlement. He knew of a house not far on the trail where an old man and his wife lived, so he turned in that direction to look for a place to sleep until morning. When he got to the house, there was nobody in it. He looked into the âsï and found no one there either. He thought maybe they had gone after water, so he stretched himself out in the farther corner to sleep. Very soon he heard a raven cry outside, and a little while afterwards the old man came into the âsï and sat down by the fire without noticing the young man, who kept still in the dark corner. Soon there was another raven cry outside, and the old man said to himself, "Now my wife is coming," and sure enough, in a little while the old woman came in and sat down by her husband. Then the young man knew they were Raven Mockers. He was frightened and kept very quiet.

Said the old man to his wife, "Well, what luck did you have?"

"None," said the old woman, "there were too many doctors watching. What luck did you have?"

"I got what I went for," said the old man. "There is no reason to fail, but you never have luck. Take this, cook it, and let us have something to eat."

She fixed the fire, and then the young man smelled meat roasting and thought it smelled sweeter than any meat he had ever tasted. He peeped out from one eye, and it looked like a man's heart roasting on a stick. Suddenly the old woman said to her husband, "Who is over in the corner?"

"Nobody," said the old man.

"Yes, there is," said the old woman, "I hear him snoring," and she stirred the fire until it blazed and lighted up the whole place, and there was the young man lying in the corner. He kept quiet and pretended to be asleep. The old man made a noise at the fire to wake him, but still he pretended to sleep. Then the old man came over and shook him, and he sat up and rubbed his eyes as if he had been asleep all the time.

Now it was near daylight, and the old woman was out in the other house, getting breakfast ready, but the hunter could hear her crying to herself.

"Why is your wife crying?" he asked the old man.

"Oh, she has lost some of her friends lately and feels lonesome," said her husband; but the young man knew that she was crying because he had heard them talking.

When they came out to breakfast, the old man put a bowl of corn mush before him and said, "This is all we have—we have had no meat for a long time."

After breakfast, the young man started on again, but when he had gone a little way, the old man ran after him with a fine piece of beadwork and gave it to him, saying, "Take this, and don't tell anybody what you heard last night, because my wife and I are always quarreling that way."

The young man took the piece, but when he came to the first creek, he threw it into the water and then went on to the settlement. There he told the whole story, and a party of warriors started back with him to kill the Raven Mockers. When they reached the place, it was seven days after the first night. They found the old man and his wife lying dead in the house, so they set fire to it, burning it and the witches together.

I was unable to find any sightings, but the creature is a shapeshifter.

ALABAMA WHITE THANG

The Alabama White Thang is described as six to seven feet, with a white-hair-covered body, and is bipedal. The creature is believed to be a cousin of Bigfoot. The Alabama White Thang has a major difference to Bigfoot; people claim that if you see an Alabama White Thang, someone has passed away. It has been a staple for

Alabama since the early 1900s and has been seen around Morgan, Etowah, and Jefferson Counties. White Thang is known for its incredible speed, lurking around in the dark; it can stand on two legs and runs on all fours; there are claims that it sounds like a screaming woman and has a foul odor like that of a dead animal. The creature's appearance sounds scary; any report of it attacking people has not been confirmed.

I have an encounter that was sent to me from a good guy named Danny Barnwell.

DANNY BARNWELL

I saw the Alabama White Thang in 1970 when I was 17 years old. Years later, my pastor, an elderly man, told me about an encounter his friend had in the 1930's at the same place. Then, in the 1990's a 90-year-old man told me of an encounter on the same mountain when he was young. All three encounters were in the same area, the exact same description, and the same reaction by the observer. The place is Hurricane Mountain, east of Jacksonville, AL. I believe that the original sightings can be traced to this mountain.

BIGFOOT

B igfoot is the king of the cryptids. Bigfoot has been seen in every state and in every country around the world. Bigfoot's history goes back as far as human history. Early histories of the North American tribes have stories of the bipedal creature. Description of Bigfoot varies depending on age and sex, but all have large feet, long arms, no visible neck, are muscular, very agile, with incredible speed, eyes that glow yellow or red, and are covered with hair which ranges from black, brown, gray, and even reddish. The full-grown males are from seven to twelve feet tall and able to run down a deer, as well as strong enough to jam a grown tree upside down into the ground. These creatures are intelligent.

There are many theories about Bigfoot, everything from being the descendants of ancient giants, interdimensional creatures, aliens, or a descendant of the *Gigantopithecus*.

The creature was introduced to the mainstream in 1958. Jerry Crew, a logging company bulldozer operator in Humboldt County, California, discovered a set of large sixteen-inch (four hundred ten millimeters) humanlike footprints sunk deep in the mud in the Six Rivers National Forest. A plaster cast was made from the prints, and he contacted a reporter from the *Humboldt Times* named Andrew Genzoli. The story came out, and news spread rapidly throughout the world.

You really can't talk about Bigfoot without mentioning the Patterson-Gimlin film in 1967. The film was shot by Roger Patterson during an expedition in Bluff Creek, Northern California. They found the creature (nicknamed Patty) by accident behind a giant root ball. The creature came into sight, surprising Patterson, and he almost fell getting off his horse, and he grabbed his camera and started filming. Gimlin rode his horse to the right of Patterson, keeping an eye on the creature. They watched the creature go across the creek bed and up a mountain. This is the most scrutinized film in history. Professional filmmakers, make-up effect artists, costumers, and film analysts have proven it's real; it has even been converted to 4K and stabilized.

I have some great encounters from nineteen amazing people.

KELLY PETROSKY

Clinton, PA

Sitting on my porch at 2 am and heard knocking on trees and it went one for half hour then a tree fell, and I live in the country with a lot of woods around me! It was very eerie, and I felt like I was being watched!

SUSAN SAVATOVIC

At first, I wasn't sure if people would be interested because it happened about 1962 when I was about 12. The event was seared in my brain and I've hidden it all these years because I thought people wouldn't believe it or think I imagined it. But if you read each version all the details are pretty much come out the same. There's not much more for me to say about what happened because I always tried to recall exactly what happened when I was 12. No embellishments.

I didn't know what I saw until the Patterson Gimlin film was all over the national news when I was 17. Only the creature that found me in the Forest was not a bulky beautiful specimen like Patty. He was a leaner sinewy version. I thought gorilla man approached me. I had no reference as to what he was but knew it was impossible that gorillas roam the forests of northern WI.

JAMES HUTCHINSON

We were camped in a place called leatherwood. The area itself is under water now covered by R.D Bailey Lake. At that time, the closest house was probably 5 miles and very few. My grandfather's house was torn down about the same year 1971. An animal kept pilfering or groceries they were in an old army tent with no bottom. The place was beautiful and covered with white sand an area the size of several football fields. It had an artisan well that came crystal clear. Everything needed to survive was there. There were cliffs with caves my dad repelled and went inside he described it as some bones and what appeared to be like something had been scooted out and pushed in the river about 190 feet below him. There's about 40 feet of the cliff still protrude from the lake. This night we had a fire like most nights and as it gets later steam raises off the water so best guess well after 11 PM. I was determined to catch whatever this was, so we set up late. I heard rattling of can food, so I ask Andy to get the lantern we came round the canvas tent myself Andy, and Olin he was at the rear this creature stood erect from a squatted position holding a loaf of bread. It was about 4 or 5 foot tall. Was covered in hair and in the light it looked grey. It looked slender built to me. There was a small cliff to its back about 10 to 12 feet tall, so I assumed it was boxed in. It scaled it in a blink. In the excitement Andy had stuck the Coleman lantern to my leg I still have the scar. I don't know how good of a look they got. but I've never forgotten it and no more encounters for nearly 50 years. now they're stripping an area called big branch. Thus, I'm looking for answers. my friends the Reverend Tommy Goode and his stepson Jeffrey a retired army veteran encountered it last year. Jeff shot several times with a 45 he was shaken and bleeding from going through briar thickets in the dark. This man is tough he has been in active duty. He also kept a round for himself. all these years this haunts me I've been a taxidermist since the 80s this thing has an anatomy unlike anything I've encountered.

Yes, sir if you google R. D Bailey Lake in Wyoming Wv. look at the small channels of the lake you will see leatherwood.

As of lately this creature is very active my friend Paul had a large stone thrown at his car, he, and his wife. It busted the tire and he had to change rim.

Bobby Dalton and Eric Kinser both armed were charged about 2 months ago and an A.E.P man said he was charged in the head of Baileysville but he doesn't want his name involved. Said it scared the crap out of him and he was in the truck.

I started to set a choker snare with 1/4 steel cables, but I don't want to kill it now. I would love to have protection for it.

I hope the rock in pic was lobbed breaking tree tops 20 feet off the ground the darn thing weighs a good 200 pounds. And I know before you say a word never

heard of a rock this size being thrown and this is Not the one thrown at Paul's car that happened about a mile above this one.

James Hutchinson
Active 1 hour ago

More

Edit

Look close at the limbs on the pine those are 10 or 12 feet up nothing could have fallen a limb etc. The other pic is a footprint, but it had to be made by a human type of creature as it is underneath the limb above it. It left several tracks about 5 feet apart and a bed about 8 feet long we found 3 in all.

Haves' good day the rock by the way we got out of road so a car wouldn't hit it. I took pics of where it came from also.

1 more thing for scale the guy in pic is kind a homeless and small in stature at 5 feet tall and 120 pounds. I have discovered it is virtually impossible to use pics they shed so little light on the facts.

DAVID PARKER

My name is David Parker and live in Northern Missouri. I been dealing with a family of Bigfoot for the past decade, I learned to live in peace with them. There are around 20 of them in all.

I tried to learn all I could but the information more speculation and BS than any real facts everyone is hoaxing and making up stories. So, I reached out to them.

I am very brave and will take out snacks for them in the evening when I hear the calls by the pond. I carry out a coffee can of goodies they want calling to them with no light or gun.

This story did happen and its tragic and hard for me to tell. When this Covid stuff began I had a friend in Canada named Kristina. Life had dealt her a cruel hand. At 26 she was terminal with Leukemia.

Ok now it gets a bit woo I believe they are telepaths and the reason for that is I had one communicating to me in my dreams. It seemed so real, but can you be 100% sure. I had heard of a group of Bigfoot that had healed a woman who had cancer.

I even spoke with an eyewitness who was there.

So, are the Bigfoot Nephilim? Not sure we will ever know for sure but anyway I could hear the females by the pond. Maybe they will mind speak to me. I have to try.

The Barn is on top of the hill that extends like a finger of land.

The pond is to the west of the barn and the dam lines up with the north side.

Never an exact location as I have had people sneaking around in the dark with night vision.

I am in northern Missouri near the Iowa border.

ok now as I am going out there, I have no light or gun and it seemed there was not a lot of moonlight.

I am walking to the barn and there is a rather large juvenile flanking me to my right Estimate him to be 10 ft tall and could see the eyeshine.

AAs I rounded the barn I heard a wood knock from near the pond as a second juvenile male came up to flank my other side. So, I get to the edge of the barn I heard 2 wood knocks from the northwest and another from the northeast. By this time, the 5 females are sounding very much like excited chimpanzees, and I tough I heard a baby cry.

So, I am on top of the hill and turn to face the females.

I have 4 juvenile males surrounding me in a box formation they are about 50 ft apart from each other with me in the center. Letting me know I am close enough they range in size from 7 ft to 10 ft in height.

So, I extended my arms and showed them open palms.

I said I am not here for that, and it was like a calming effect went over them all.

I was not afraid as my mind was set on the task to try to communicate.

So, I began by speaking aloud and using sign to try to see if they could or would mind speak with me as I related what I was asking.

It failed maybe because I was trying to force it. Tears were rolling down my cheeks as I had failed.

Then I heard a big male howling with the coyotes and thought maybe it was up to him so, I turned and walked past 2 of the juveniles like they were not even there to go to where the big one was. I could not see him but could smell him. I tried again with the same results I went in the house. Kris has since passed but as na man I had to try. I would have not been able to face myself had I not tried.

It happened and I hope you can use it.

My wife had an encounter today and posted in my group.

One of the younger females did mind speak to her.

They like her.

A life with Bigfoot is the group. People need to hear stories that are not all scary.

Really, they are fairly harmless unless you try to harm one.

GLEN BOURASSA

I was going camping with my brother and meeting at the camp. I was 20 or 30 minutes ahead of him coming from a different direction, so I just started looking for a place to pull off the road and look around. I saw this small path to my left and had to back up to drive down. It was just an old turn around and was very muddy in spots. I looked from inside the Toyota rav4 and saw a smaller path that hadn't been used for years so I went that way. As I passed this huge tree, I saw a tree had fallen a few years back and was partially cut up. I pulled forward and I see this 'pitcher top right' so I get out and look and I see hair all over the ground no bones but thick hair covering a 20 x 8-foot area. Then I noticed a huge plop of shit and a smaller plop next to it. 'Pitcher bottom left ' the smaller one is next to a leaf that was bigger than my hand. Then I started looking at it sticks and how it was constructed, and I'm amazed. Nothing cut and woven almost. So, I need to meet my brother, so I go. After we set up part of the camp, I bring him to look. He is also very perplexed. He didn't want to go deeper into the mountain laurels to have a look. So, the week I bring a friend AJ and hike around. We almost got lost a few times in the laurels but didn't find much that day. AJ and I did a few night investigation but didn't have much going on, a lot of background noise from the freeway a couple hundred yards away. One day I took AJ Grabosky, Stephanie, and her old boyfriend to the spot to hike farther down into the laurels. We had hike for a couple hours and I discussed letting this area cool down for a while and everyone agreed so we hiked out and drove to a more popular public hiking trail and went down to the creek looking for evidence as always. On the way down I saw a tiny stick structure all the sticks were 8 or 9 inches long and amazingly put together. We keep hiking and find a small island and started looking. We came across a single footprint that was the size of a 6-year-old kid maybe. No shoe and the print were an inch deep. We keep walking and somehow came to the same footprint. So I took the lead and we hiked out because it was getting dark. We drove back to the 1st area and because it was muddy and dark I decided to back in. We had been talking and I ask Stephanie to say a few things to put the Bigfoot at ease. She asks what to say I explained just talk say hello and she did for a few minutes. Maybe a half hour later I didn't have a flashlight at the time but I walked to our right toward the laurels and the other's had the lights on my back. I noticed how big of a shadow I was casting on the laurels. I started talking like I had asked Stephanie to do for a couple minutes then I walked back to the SUV. Maybe 15 minutes had passed and AJ had gotten into the SUV front passenger seat. And I had decided to do a Roar like I had heard in Arizona. I didn't tell anyone and as I turned, I saw that the driver window was down and didn't want to do it into his ears, so I went to the back of the driver's side of the SUV and tried to replicate what I had heard. I only did a 1 second Roar and within a half second something started stomping up at me. Branches breaking and the pounding was so loud we all felt it through the ground. AJ also inside the SUV. We all started jumping in the SUV Stephanie's ex-boyfriend jumped into the driver side back door and slammed it Stephanie had to run around the front of the SUV to get in. I started it and when she was in, I took off all 3 of them where yelling doesn't stop that thing could knock this SUV over go. After we got a mile away, I wanted to go back but didn't want anything to happen to anyone. So, the next morning AJ Grabosky and I went back. we found some Branches 3 inches across broken and toss throughout some of the laurels.

My 2nd encounter I was leaving my friend's house going to rainbow lake and his dog was walking ahead of me. We heard the same Roar the dog stopped and looked back at me and took off running towards the sound as fast as I could looking up in trees side to side. I came to the clearing of the lake I was out of breath and decided to go to the right at an angle to the lake edge. I was walking along the edge and noticed something 50 yards away looked like mud above the ground. As I got closer, I see it's a footprint going into the lake it was huge only the front half of the foot 8 inches deep and 7 inches wide when it stepped it pushed the mud up over 15 inches and was curved back towards the shore. I got this calm feeling of knowing. 3rd encounter to follow.

My 3rd encounter with Bigfoot.!!! I had been drinking a bottle of wine with a friend Peggy to be exact. The same Peggy from the 1st encounter. After we finished the bottle, I asked if she could take the empty with her because I wanted to investigate the other side of the creek because I had never looked on that side. We said goodbye and I walked over to the creek looking for a place to cross. I found a spillway about 18 inches wide, and I crossed. I stayed about 20 yards from the water and made my way along, I had walked maybe 150 yards and I see fresh breaks on a thick stick holding the barbed wire fence. So, I go closer to get a look and I see a clump of blonde hair stuck on the top of the barbed wire. It was 5 inches long and the clump was the size of my middle finger. I was 2 feet away from it studying it when all the hair on my neck stood up and I could tell something was watching

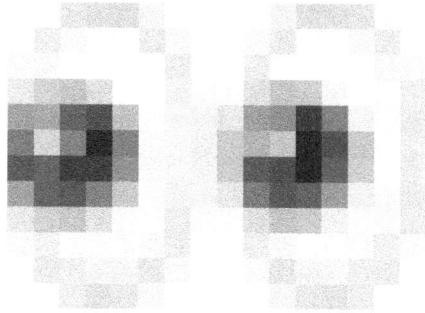

me. I did a 360 and dropped to the ground like Spiderman and looked around and slowly backed away for 5 feet then slowly got back on my feet and walked away slowly. As I got back to the spillway I was thinking if it was down on the deep side of the spillway it could have grabbed me and I would never have been seen again. It was getting dark, so I went home. The next morning, I tool a friend with me to show him and look for more evidence. We to the spot and the hair was gone. I couldn't believe it just gone. I was looking on the ground for hair or prints when my friend for some reason turned a large rock up on its end and under that rock was tangled up barbed wire. No human would do that only 20 feet from the deep creek they would just toss it into the creek or take it with them. And no other animals can do this except for Bigfoot.

ANTHONY SHIELDS

My name is Anthony and I've been a serious sasquatch researcher for going on 8 years now and have had a lifelong interest in the topic. I work with the public, and it was 8 years ago that a long-time client of mine revealed that he had seen one in the 80s out of his crop dusting plane along the Kansas Oklahoma border and I undoubtedly believe his story. It was his recount of his experience that took me from armchair interested to full-blown researcher in the months and years to follow. I now have thousands of dollars invested in equipment, hundreds of hours under my belt, handfuls of exchanges on the topic with peers scattered around the country whom I exchange information with. A few years back I got my first bite, here's a little backstory to that. I'm not afraid to ask questions and seek answers when out in the field to save time and streamline the process. So, whenever I encounter a warden, Ranger or even random bait and tackle shop operator I'll ask some probing questions. Two years prior to my what we'll call "encounter" in the Mark Twain national forest, I had spoken to a forest ranger in the area that had an interesting tale that had lingered through his forestry department over the years. He came by our campsite to check and make sure that our tags were on our 4 wheelers and dirt bikes, a fee needs to be paid to ride in this portion of the Mark Twain national Forest and this is how they check that fees have been paid. While having breakfast noticed him pull up outside my RV window and start walking towards my trailer and knew he was just there to check the tags. I couldn't resist the opportunity to squeeze in some questions. I hopped outside and asked him if there had been any sightings in the area. After some probing he mentioned that some of the what he called "old-timers" had told him stories about a family of them back in the 80s being viewed on a farm that hubs up against the Mark Twain national Forest. Basically he said that sometime back in the 80s a farmer kept calling into fish and game saying that some large animal kept coming onto his property killing chickens, stealing fruits and vegetables etc. They gave him permission to put out a bear trap and he called back a week later hysterical saying that he had trapped some sort of gorilla and to get out there immediately. According to this Rangers story some people from the forest department showed up out there, and there stood a family of three of them. A large male, a female and a juvenile that had its foot caught in the bear trap (chained around the base of a fruit tree) it was screaming hysterically. The adult sasquatch seemingly keeping guard over it while attempting to figure out how to free it from the trap. The rangers knew their guns weren't big enough to do much damage and apparently didn't know exactly what to do with such creatures, so they called in local law-enforcement. He didn't specify if it was state patrol or local police who arrived first but as they came down the road with their sirens and lights blaring the large male seemingly agitated by this, turned, and yanked the trap free from the tree, chains, and all, tossed the screaming juvenile over his shoulder and the three of them retreated into the forest. As someone who's worked with the public for over 20 years and converses with random people day to day I've got a pretty good BS meter. I don't think this guy was pulling my leg, he seemed a little bit in disbelief himself. He concluded the conversation with, "so be careful out here at night"… That brings us to my encounter that happened earlier a few years back,

2 years after hearing the story from this Ranger. Primarily focusing my research in the Ouachita Mountains of Oklahoma and Arkansas (nearest hot spot to where I lived at the time, Kansas. I recently moved to Arizona), I had only done light research in the past in the Mark Twain national forest in Missouri(some wood knocks and late night hikes while vacationing) I decided after the story it was time to up my game a little bit, put out some bait cameras and go a little deeper into the forest, a little darker a little later at night. So mid-June of 2018, my son and wife ready to retire to the RV after a day of riding in the forest, I loaded up my little dog Remi, my thermal image camera, infrared camera, bear mace and high-power spotlight, got on the four-wheeler and headed off into the forest towards the depths. It started off with wood knocks about 20/30 minutes into my trek (few miles from camp, pitch black forest at this point) I heard them having stopped to investigate an interesting looking black fox that had ran in front of my 4-wheeler. I killed the motor and the forest sounds soon resumed. I heard two sets of them. About a mile apart from each other and a little over half mile from my location. They were clearly communicating with each other. This was not someone chopping wood, or a woodpecker. If it was people doing it they would have to be incredibly strong as one of the knocks even though traveling a great distance still sent slight reverberations through my body. It was a big piece of wood hitting another very big piece of wood, in a rhythmic pattern, repeatedly over time, sometimes with several minutes of silence in between. At this point in time, I was in the middle of the forest, it was about 1 AM and the area that the sounds were coming from was uninhabited. Dense thick brush, trees, cliffs, mountains etc. I stopped and listened for some time. Out of all the technology I had, I didn't have a parabolic ear with me (I've since gotten one). I tried my best to record with my phone and you don't really hear much over the sounds of the crickets and frogs in the foreground. I made an attempt to quiet those sounds by clapping and making some loud hush sounds, the bugs would quiet briefly and quickly return, seemingly the wood knocking stopped during those hushed periods as well. Frustrated after about 20 minutes of this and not being able to capture good audio I decided to venture on. Went about an hour's distance further into the forest at an idle speed (unknowingly, I didn't realize until later, I was headed towards the direction of the first set of knocks I had heard) when I noticed a powerline cutting through the dense forest across the trail ahead of me. With powerlines come tree breaks and with tree breaks come easy animal thoroughfares. I knew this would be a good place to spotlight. Now here's where it starts to get weird. It's worth mentioning I'm not afraid of the dark and if I was, I've picked the wrong hobby. I grew up in Nebraska late night cat fishing and later cow tipping, night hiking and camping in my teen years and I don't scare easily in a dark forest. In a strange way it's a comfort zone for me, but this was different. As I approached the powerline/tree break I heard my little dog start to whimper in the backseat, something she doesn't do. She's small but she's the first one at the door and at your ankles when you come to my house. One of those little yippy thinks she's 500 pounds dogs. So, she starts whimpering and at the same time every hair on my entire body stands up on end. Not just the hair on the back of my neck, the hair on my arms, knuckles, legs, I could even feel the hair on my toe tops struggling against my socks. I slowed my idle and took my hand off the gas completely and readied my spotlight, unable to shake this creepy feeling that had quickly came over me. I look to the left and almost thankfully don't see anything; I quickly pan to my right and there it is. Whatever it is. It's about 50 yards away from me, roughly 8/9 feet tall, taking up a large black space amongst the space between the trees and brush. Like a large cave shaped doorway. Now 50 yards and as high powered of a spotlight as I had, I should have seen this thing as plain as day, but I couldn't see it. My light lit up everything around it and its eyes reflected my light, but I could not see the actual physical creature itself. No details. just Black. The eyes seemed startled at first upon my light striking it, then the eyes sneered in a way as to try to squint past the light, ducking briefly and then returning to the original height before slowly stepping sideways out of the line of sight, smoothly, calmly, and quietly. It really seemed as though this thing was standing there expecting to sneak a peek at me coming by (it could have heard my motor from some distance slowly coming down the trail) and seemed startled and frustrated that it had been lit up. While fumbling for my thermal camera to get an image to be completely honest fear and the instinct of self-preservation took over and I sped on down the road a way to gather my bearings. Like I said, I've been out in some pretty thick stuff solo several times, have stumbled upon large bucks, packs of coyotes, bumped my head against roosting turkeys etc. It takes a lot to startle me and whatever the hell this thing had seemingly affected me on an instinctual level, something I wasn't quite prepared for. In the future I will always have a pistol on me and preferably a sidekick of some kind to help man cameras, lights etc. Having only 2 hands and 10 things to do didn't fare well in the field... Eventually I got my gumption back up and raced back past the area to return to camp as it was the only way back to camp. Never saw the thing again but it's worth mentioning I felt something yet again as I passed that area and for some time afterwards. I did not see any signs of this but rather felt it, it felt like the thing followed me out to make sure I was gone. It seemed like it kept just behind enough to stay out of the sight of my brake lights. I was too freaked out to kill the motor to listen, so I just kept moving but I had that feeling with me for some distance. The following day I returned to the area with my wife and son and noticed a clear large open pathway of sorts through the thick brush, no actual animal trail however created by hooves or anything like that, just matted down brush where some-thing large had matted down a walkway. Lots of berries in the area and a stream within 20 yards and mountainous cliffs ascending to impenetrable terri-tory just beyond that. Something comes down out of those mountains at night and eats at those berries, it does it with enough regularity to create a pathway, it does not have hooves, it is 8/9 feet tall and dark enough to soak up the light from a spotlight. It is alive and does have eyeballs that reflect light. That I know. There it is, my closest so far encounter. This wasn't a conclusion for me as much as it was a lesson on how to be better prepared in the future. I don't want to BS myself or others, I have no desire for that, and I don't claim that every bump in the night is a bigfoot. When I know, I really want to know. Covid hit and my small business crashed. I've relocated to Arizona and have recently acquired a Polaris Ranger capable of getting back into the thick of it and doing some scouting & camping. I'm currently researching accounts in the Arizona, New Mexico region and plan on shifting my research to those areas in the upcoming months. I eventually plan on spending a great deal of time in the Pacific Northwest later in life to put in some miles there. This hobby covers a lot of territory and there's only so much time. Feel free to reach out if you have any questions. I'm full of information, most of it useless lol.

JAMES "BOBO" FREY

I remember it like it was yesterday, 26 years ago on September 21st, 1997, I was sitting on the couch after letting my dogs hotdog and hamdog outside to go potty when I heard this deep growl almost sounding like someone revving an engine so I went to check it out and I barely made it off my porch when I saw his huge squatch holding my hamdog in his mouth! I immediately ran inside and locked the door, but I could still hear the creature outside feasting on my poor baby dogs. the next morning, I went outside to find the skeletons of hotdog and hamdog licked clean and that's what started my curiosity of the sasquatch.

JAMI PETERS

August 11 1987 my family and myself was camping on the little birch river in Braxton County WV we had just finished breakfast outside under the pines on a picnic table the ladies had cleaned up and done the dishes and was preparing to go for a hike and go fishing a daily ritual we were all outside when all the sudden my aunt Carolyn screamed omg look every one turned to see and there it was coming from the river it walked fast across our camp in broad day light about 60 yards from us it never looked toward us or paid attention to our barking dog patches my uncle jumped on his ATV a 225 Yamaha mor04 and tried to catch up with it but once it hit the tree line it was gone in 6 steps, until this hour I did not believe in bigfoot I considered it a wise tail parents used to get kids in before dark.

KEVIN L. PETERSON JR.

I saw what I guess you would call it a toddler Bigfoot on my second of two encounters. I was wearing camouflage sitting about 20ft off the ground deer hunting when all of a sudden, I heard something bipedal loudly walking through the woods. I believed it to be my cousin coming to hunt the stand I was in. I turned my head and upper body towards the noise much to my surprise I saw an approximately 7 1/2ft tall around 500lbs hairy creature that froze in place looking at me. After a few seconds it let out a large loud huff noise at this point a smaller one around 2ft hard to estimate the weight stepped out from behind a tree and climbed onto the back of the larger one. It was quick and nimble reminded me of a baby chimp climbing over its mother only more human. After what seemed like minutes but was probably only 40 seconds the big one started to back away from me without ever taking its eyes off me the little one just clung there looking straight away. Once this thing was around 30 yards from me it was like it just vanished into thin air the way it blended back into the woods.

DON S. KINDRED

September 1970, I was backpacking in Desolation Wilderness, southwest of Lake Tahoe. I was 21 and recently out of the service. I was with 3 other guys on a 5-day lake hopping trip. We set up camp at Susie Lake on our last night of a successful backpacking excursion.

After dinner we were sitting around the campfire sipping on hot tea. (No drugs or alcohol on the trip) We had a young German Shepard with us that was well behaved but loved chasing everything that moved. Suddenly a large rock land in our campsite. Then another and another landed in the campsite. These rocks were up to 6 inches in diameter. We saw no other campers or campfires on the lake, so we figured some guys were just screwing with us. I took the dog and a flashlight and went in the direction the rocks were coming from. I found no sign of anyone, so I came back to camp. The rocks stopped coming so we dismissed the incident and bedded down for the night. We had no tent and just slept by the campfire.

At 2:05 am I was woken by the sound of backpackers coming down the trail toward us. I heard them talking. The closer they got, their talking sounded garbled and nonsensical. We had a full moon that night. I leaned up on my elbow to see who was coming down the trail. They came into view and continued walking towards us. Two huge creatures stopped in front of us. Just the dog and I were awake. I was staring at them, and they were staring at me. The one on the right was about 8 feet tall and covered in very dark hair. It had a leathery face with sunken eyes, a flat nose, and a somewhat protruding forehead. Assuming this was a male, his shoulders were extremely wide and arms longer than a human. The one on the left was about 7 feet tall and had light colored hair and similar features. I was frozen in my sleeping bag as they just stared at me. I felt totally vulnerable. I was also concerned about our skittish dog who was laying against my sleeping bag. She was frozen with her ears back and hair standing straight up. She too was staring but didn't move.

After about 2 minutes of us staring at each other, they both walked over to the creek nearby, stooped down and drank water by cupping their hands. Then the larger one climbed up a small tree and brought something in his right hand when he came down. I have no idea what was in his hand. Then they walked across the creek and out of sight.

I stayed awake and motionless until daybreak as I was concerned, they were still around. Then I woke up the guys and told them what happened. They didn't believe me. I went to the creek where they drank water and crossed and saw clear footprints. I showed them the footprints, but they still didn't believe any of it. We had no iPhones back in the day and no camera on this trip. I paced off the distance where they were standing, and it was 32 feet from where I was laying in my sleeping bag.

A few years after the encounter, I was encouraged to write this experience to Rene Dahinden, a well-known Bigfoot author of the day. He wrote back asking if I would be willing to film my experience. Based on the fact that no one believed me, I declined.

At age 21, the word Bigfoot wasn't on my radar. I knew nothing about such a creature. I have no doubt of what I saw and as terrified as I was, I thought these creatures were magnificent. That's my story and this is the first time I've published it.

CURT BRUEGGEMAN

Hi, my name is Curt. I'm 46 years old and have lived in Minnesota for the past 25 years. I grew up southwestern Wisconsin and had lived there until age twenty. In 1976, when I was thirteen, there were a couple of reported bigfoot sightings in a small town south of us called Cashton. From that moment on I started reading books and watching television programs related to bigfoot. From then on, I have been fascinated with the subject, and am convinced that bigfoot exists. There's way too many claimed bigfoot sightings for all of them to be dismissed as bear or other animal sightings. Most recently I've been frequenting a couple of Bigfoot websites reading all of their stories.

I have an eighteen-year-old son whose nickname has been Bear since birth. Every so often I would tell him about some bigfoot sighting stories that I had heard or read about. He insisted that they were a "Mythical Creature" that didn't exist because there was no place in North America for them to hide. He also said that someone by now would have shot or trapped one for everybody to see. Bear went through his first year of boot camp last year where they went on numerous nighttime reconnaissance maneuvers. He's familiar with the woods and all of the more common animals that live there, and has also been deer hunting for a few years.

My family of five has been camping since about 1992. All locations have been at your typical campgrounds, but a couple of them were more remote sites at State or County campgrounds. We've seen many different animals during hikes through the woods. Mostly small animals, but we have on a couple of occasions seen a bear. It may sound trivial, but we have seen monkeys, gorillas, moose, elk, and lots of other animals at the Minnesota state zoo.

I have been considering going hiking and camping in the wilderness in an attempt to look for bigfoot for years, but have never followed through with it. I had been surfing the web when I came across this web-site that offered bigfoot expeditions at different times of the year in different states. So a few months back I contacted the Wisconsin state bigfoot representative and filled out the required paperwork. Bear and I were now set up to attend a bigfoot expedition which was going to take place in north central Wisconsin from Thursday May 7th, 2009, through Sunday May 10th, 2009.

Thursday May 7th, 2009:

On Thursday afternoon at 2:30pm, after weeks of getting all of our camping equipment ready and packed followed by a three-and-a-half-hour drive, Bear and I arrived at the rural home of a lifelong Wisconsin resident who is also a professional guide and hunter. I learned that he has had numerous encounters with what he believes is a family of four bigfoot. He routinely takes daytime and nighttime hikes through this nearby wilderness area where we would be camping. I believe he also deer hunts in the same location.

At approximately 3:30 pm we followed our guide to a base camp that he had identified as the most likely spot for bigfoot activity. This camp was approximately a forty yard by seventy yard clearing in the woods just off of the gravel road that led us there. The wooded area that we were in is part of a county forest that has hundreds of miles of logging roads. The terrain was relatively flat with a few small hills thrown in between numerous lowlands, with small lakes to our south and east. Further away a river wraps around our east and south sides, and an extremely large bog lies just to our north. Some distance to our west were three or four rural homes, some of which had horses. Gradually over the next few hours, more and more people started showing up. All total, there were between twenty-five and thirty people attending the expedition. Ages ranged from seventeen to sixty something. In attendance were about eight active and former military personnel, about seven bigfoot investigators, the head of the Bigfoot Research Organization (BFRO), and the rest of us were either first-timers or experienced expeditioners. People came from

Wisconsin, Minnesota, Illinois, Michigan, Florida, North Carolina, and California.

At approximately 5:00pm, led by our tracker, all of us went hiking around as a group to familiarize ourselves with the old logging paths. Hundreds of game trails crisscrossed and paralleled our path as we went exploring. We would routinely step off the main path to analyze a few of these game trails to determine the size of the animals that were frequenting them. During our hike about six or eight places were identified as locations that would be manned for our first nights mission. A couple of hours after hiking in a large clockwise pattern that covered approximately one square mile, we found ourselves back at base camp.

Sitting around the base campfire, Mr. BFRO told us of many incidences that he was either a part of, or heard of while leading an expedition. Our tracker also shared his encounters that he's had over the years. Besides an extremely rare day time bigfoot sighting, people would claim to hear whooping noises, whistling noises, wood knocks, smelling a musty wet-dog like odor, and seeing red or yellow glowing eyes. We were also told of the bigfoots curiosity with humans who would enter the areas in which they existed.

We were instructed to have our FRS radios on channel 3 at all times, as we would be at specified locations during the evening. Any sounds we heard could be communicated and pinpointed by as many groups as possible. The radios could also be used in case of an emergency. Then we were introduced to the hi-tech viewing/recording devices that we would all be sharing. Four or five night-vision goggles were handed out. These were similar to binoculars in that you look into them with both eyes, but only one viewing tube came out of the other side. Many of us have seen these in movies or have used them as was the case with our military personnel. When you look through them everything is green. You can see whatever you are pointing at just like it was almost daytime. You could easily see the path and the surrounding area, but when looking into the dense woods at night you were limited to about twenty or thirty feet of vision.

Then there were the infrared devices. They came in three different styles. The hand-held monocular style that you hold up to one eye. The hand-held or tripod held style that looks like a large SLR digital camera and comes in recording and a non-recording versions. And the R2D2 style that sits on the roof of a vehicle. It was controlled by a joystick inside or close to the vehicle. It had a Sony digital video camera connected to it that was used to both view and record. It also had the capability of rotating 360 degrees and tilting up or down. Thermal devices can see in the dark similar to night vision except everything is a differing shade of white or grey. The hotter the temperature of the target, the brighter white it appears on the screen. These can see for hundreds of yards. A person can pick up the heat from a mouse at 50 yards or a bear at a quarter mile away. Their only limitation was that the heat signature was hard to identify from long distances. You could identify a person walking at 400 yards, but if they were just sitting there, you would only know that it was a live target. You may have seen these used on the show Cops. The police helicopters would help locate a fugitive in the woods because his body temperature would give him away.

Sometime around midnight, we all started scattering through the woods and swamps towards our designated locations. Some of us would be stationary while others would be mobile. The moon was full and bright. Hiking was very easy as we had more than enough light to see our paths. We started out as a group of about nine, but shortly broke off into a group of four as we were walking faster than the group watching the thermal camera. After about half an hour or so, someone announced that they were going to make some whooping noises south of base camp in the next ten seconds. We all stopped and waited. My particular group was unfortunate enough to stop near a whippoorwill that had apparently drank too much red bull. Then we heard the whoops and waited for any replies. After a couple of seconds, we heard one or two coyotes start yelping to our southeast. Some groups on the far west end heard yelping but couldn't identify the source because of their distance. We confirmed that what they heard were definitely coyotes. Someone later did some wood knocks, but we got no response from anything. We walked and stopped numerous times over the next ninety minutes or so before we were all told to come back to base camp to wrap up the evening. Our group arrived around 2:30. The group behind us took a longer way around and ended up walking down the gravel road to camp. Two members of their group were about fifty yards ahead of the three others with the thermal camera. One of them identified two red glowing eyes and pointed them out to the second. They confirmed with each other that they were seeing the same thing in the same location. By the time the other three showed up with the thermal camera, the target had disappeared. They got back to camp around 3:30am.

Friday May 8th, 2009:

Most people slept in on Friday morning, but a few got up earlier and made the ten-to-fifteen-mile drive to town for breakfast. Bear and I woke up around 11:30am. We slept in the back of our GMC Yukon and awoke to the sensation of being baked like a cake. This was due to the hot sun now shining on our vehicle. We opened the doors to a nice cool breath of fresh air and then got out to put our shoes on. We ate a couple of military meals that my son had brought and waited around the smoldering campfire ashes for our scheduled 2:00pm meeting to discuss the previous night's activities. The discussion centered around the eye-shine that the two gentlemen had seen only a few hours earlier. After walking the quarter mile west of camp, we came to the location where the eye-shine occurred. From there we did some more exploring of the area to check out some potential hot spots for activity later that night. Some of us continued exploring, and some went back to camp to rest before our scheduled 7:00pm planning meeting.

It was decided that my truck would be equipped with the R2D2 thermal device. A young woman, who I'll call "Rosie," volunteered to operate it from the passenger seat once we had our remote campsite set up. The temperature was expected to drop down to around forty degrees, so I wore extra clothes under my jeans and black wool coat. Rosie did the same and covered up with her full military issue camo gear and hat. Since Bear was planning on laying on the ground in the woods fully dark, he wore three layers of everything under his full body military green rain suit. He was equipped with night vision and thermal devices and was prepared to lay there all night.

At about 8:15pm we arrived at our planned location west of base camp. It was right on the west side of the road where there was eye-shine the previous night. The field we were in was about a quarter mile long and paralleled the road going north and south. It was approximately four hundred yards deep going west. It had been logged sometime in the past few years and was littered with dried up scrap wood. I positioned my vehicle on the north end just about twenty yards south of the tree line. Directly in my sight was a path that extended approximately four hundred yards to the north. I parked there because we were going to put Bear down that path for the night. We first gathered some of the dead wood and made a campfire. Daylight was rapidly turning to dusk as Bear, and I started walking north along the path to his bed for the night. We went in about one hundred and seventy-five yards and met two other guys who were planning on being in the same area. I didn't want them too close to each other, so they decided to go back a little ways and lay a couple of yards off the east side of the trail. I told Bear to walk down about twenty yards off the west side of the trail. In front of him he had a good line of sight to a saw grass infested swamp. The swamp was only about fifteen yards deep and about forty yards long. I told him that if he needed me just to yell "DAD" on the radio, and I'd be there in a flash. I worked my way back to the path and on up to the truck. I say up because I was going up a slight incline even though I was heading south.

Upon returning, Rosie had the fire going pretty good and had already pulled up a chair. It was fairly dark by then. I decided to hang a couple of glow sticks from some saplings for the heck of it. I hung the green one approximately two hundred and fifty yards south of the truck. I put some red hots candy on a stump below it. After coming back, I took the red colored stick and hung it about a hundred and fifty yards directly west of the truck. I placed two mostly eaten apples on a stump below that one. Rosie gave me a candy bar to place on a stump next to the path just north of the truck. By then it was completely dark, and Rosie had moved to the truck and started up R2D2. I sat in the chair next to the fire and relaxed for a few minutes. I keyed up the radio to ask how my little buddy was doing. In a hushed voice he said he was fine. About fifteen or twenty minutes later we had the same brief contact. The radio was quiet as no plans for whoops or knocks was supposed to take place until after midnight. It had been a little over an hour when I asked Rosie if she could see the red glow stick west of our truck through R2D2. She said she couldn't, so I told her that I would walk down there and point it out. About three quarters of the way there, the hair on my neck and arms stood up and I felt like someone was watching me from the woods just to my right. I started to whistle the rest of the way to the glow stick and pointed it out to Rosie who was watching on R2D2. I whistled all the way back to the truck. I told Rosie that that was an extremely uncomfortable walk.

It wasn't ten minutes before I heard the following on the walkie-talkie... "I GOT EYE-SHINE, I GOT EYE-SHINE!" Then "F##K THIS, I'M OUTTA HERE!" I was still outside of the vehicle at that time, and I took off on a dead sprint north towards Bears location. I met him about one hundred and fifty yards down the path. As he was running, I grabbed him and we both continued back in the direction of the truck. He was shaking uncontrollably, and he said, "THAT'S F##KED UP, DAD, NOTHING LIKE THAT SHOULD BE IN THESE WOODS. IT WAS MASSIVE!" I told him that I had him now and I wouldn't let anything hurt him. We got back to the truck where Rosie had been waiting with locked doors and her eyes on the thermal down the path. Bear jumped in the back and started taking off his gear. By then Mr. BFRO had already jumped in his vehicle and was on his way to the location of the encounter. He asked if Bear could come back and point out where he was laying. So back down the path we went. Bear had two fists full of my jacket in his hands as he was leaning on me and shaking the whole way. We met Mr. BFRO and the two other guys on the path near where Bear was originally located. Mr. BFRO wanted to know what he saw. Bear said, "I was just lying there propped up on one elbow looking around when I saw a pair of amber colored eyes, then they switched to white, and then they switched to red. I picked up the thermal and saw a MASSIVE body leaning out from behind the tree and then I said I'm outta here." Back at the truck I gave him a sleeping pill to calm him down and told Rosie to talk to him. I went back down the trail to look around with the other guys. The two gentlemen on the other side of the trail saw nothing and heard only Bear's transmission and him crashing through the brush on a mad dash to get out of the woods.

Now back in the truck, Bear was finally sleeping, and Rosie was getting tired, so she called her boyfriend to pick her up and take her back to base camp. I took over the controls of R2D2 and didn't go to sleep until dawn.

Saturday May 9th, 2009:

We both woke up around 12:30pm and had just opened the doors of the truck to put on our shoes when Mr. BFRO come flying up to our location in his truck. He told us of all the people at base camp talking about the sighting. Since we weren't back yet, they thought that we may have left in terror sometime in the middle of the night. Someone had hiked into the woods and found Bears cap and jokingly told the others that he may have been kidnapped by bigfoot and that's all that was left. Once back at base camp we discussed the previous night's encounter and decided that we should all take a walk down to where it occurred. We identified the exact locations and positions of Bear and his sighting of bigfoot. Bear was laying on the ground about thirty yards away from where bigfoot was standing. Based on the location of a branch, we estimated the bigfoot to be about seven feet six inches tall, or more if it had its legs bent. I stood in the same spot and position that bigfoot was standing in. I'm six feet four inches and weigh about two hundred and ten pounds, and my shoulder width is approximately two feet. When I asked Bear how wide the bigfoots shoulders were compared to mine, he said "at least twice as wide." We spent the next hour scouring the forest behind and next to the sighting for any possible evidence. We found nothing that was conclusive. (See attached picture).

The rest of the afternoon was spent preparing for the coming evening. We moved half of the people from base camp to an alternate location in a gravel pit. It was horseshoe shaped with sides that were about twenty-five feet high. We hid a few trail cameras around the rim of the campsite to catch anything that would have wandered in. I felt like we were surrounded, and the only way out could be easily blocked by one bigfoot.

For dinner, the wife of our professional tracker brought us chili, beans, ham sandwiches, and potato salad. It was good. We had a campfire going and it was starting to sprinkle. Some people huddled under the back hatches of their SUV's and others just sat in the rain. It didn't last long, but as the overcast night grew colder, and we needed to add more wood to the fire. We sat there for a few hours' chit chatting, and people started to waffle over what they were going to do that night. Everyone was pretty cold and tired from the previous days of the expedition. Most decided to stay at one camp or the other, and then go to bed before it got too late.

Five of us however decided that we weren't at all tired and teamed up to take a walk around 1:00am. For our adventure we brought along one night vision and one thermal device. We headed south on the gravel road which went right between the sightings from Thursday and Friday night. We walked for about a third of a mile while making frequent stops. The sound of us walking on the gravel reminded me of hearing military personnel marching, only louder. We were talking and joking and being all around loud. We took frequent breaks to stop and concentrate on our conversation, or to simply water the grass in the tree line.

At the south end of our walk, we turned east on one of the many paths we had explored in the previous days. Even though it was overcast, we still had enough light to see where we were going. A couple of hundred yards in, we found ourselves on a small hill overlooking about a half square mile of lowlands, swamps, bogs, and a small lake with a couple of tiny islands. We decided to make some whooping sounds. It was awesome how loud it was as I heard it echo about six or eight times around the whole area. We got the attention of the coyotes about a half mile east of us like we did on the first night. We hiked another couple of hundred yards and decided that we weren't ambitious enough to hike the rest of the way around the path, so we turned around. Back *on top of this hill I made a loon call which sounded really cool, but I got no response other than some wise cracks from the group. I looked around with the night vision and recognized that we were at a point in the path where we could take a shortcut back to camp. This path paralleled the gravel road but was darker because there was about fifty yards of forest between us and the road, and moon. To our east was about a quarter square mile of lowland grasses.*

From time to time one or two of us thought we would hear something in the woods, but nothing that really made us think too much. We continued to look around with the night vision and thermal as we walked. We even did a tree knock but got no responses. I took a turn with the thermal and got a heat signature across the lowland area but couldn't tell anything about it other than it was fairly good sized and was moving around pretty slow. We watched it for about ten or twelve minutes when some of us again heard a sound from the woods to the side and behind us. We decided to make a whistle sound. We made one whistle from a low pitch to a high pitch. Almost immediately we heard a loud duplicate whistle near where we had just heard the sound to the side and behind us. I estimated it to be about fifty yards away. We again panned the area with our electronics but saw nothing. A few minutes later we thought we should make another whistle. Again, almost immediately, we heard a duplicate whistle except this time it was from a few hundred yards to our west. Almost immediately following that we heard two whistles, almost at the same time, coming from a couple hundred yards to our north and to our south. We heard nothing from the area that we heard our initial whistle response fifty yards away.

After a few minutes of excited whispering and shushing between us, we decided to continue up the path. When we came to the end of our path, we decided to make a U-turn on the gravel road instead of heading back to camp. We figured that if something was following us, we might surprise it by turning around. We followed the road about a hundred yards and then walked a little way into the field where I had parked the previous night. We panned the area and one of the guys got a heat signature on the thermal from the ditch across the road. Since the ditch was only a couple of feet deep, he said it appeared as if something was crawling. Then he said that it lifted up and appeared to look around and drop back to the ground. By the time he handed the thermal to someone else to look, it was gone. We stayed there for about fifteen minutes or so, and then someone suggested we get back to camp.

We then hiked the same path that I had sprinted down just the night before. Halfway down we heard what I recalled thinking was a poor impression of an owl about forty yards to our west. Just one hoot is all that we heard. Almost immediately we heard just one hoot reply from about two hundred yards to our north. We waited in silence for a few minutes. Since we couldn't see anything on our electronics, we decided to go back to camp. We sat around the campfire whispering for about thirty minutes. About 3:30 we decided to go to bed.

Sunday May 10th, 2009

Sunday morning, we all gathered at base camp to discuss the previous evening, and then posed for a group photo and to say our goodbyes. Bear and I drove the three and a half hours back to the twin cities where we had lots of stories to reminisce about. We unloaded the vehicle as we discussed going to another bigfoot expedition.

Final Thoughts:

Mr. BFRO said that to his knowledge Bear was the only one documented to see the three different colors of glowing eyes coming from the same bigfoot. It has been thought for years that the glowing eyes are a way of communication between the bigfoots. That's quite possible, but I'd like to offer another theory. I think that as the bigfoot is wandering around the woods and they see something that they can't quite identify, they switch their vision to see better. Just like we use our normal eyes, or switch to night vision, or switch to thermal vision devices.

Another opinion I have is that regardless of whether you're quiet or noisy, wearing camo or a suit and tie, wearing cologne or not showering for a month. Bigfoot will find you by using their very sharp senses. There's nothing you can do to hide. I recommend not trying to be stealthy or dressing in orange. I think a bigfoot is intelligent enough to determine that they are seeing a hunter, or whether they are watching a bunch of loud, potty-mouthed, joke telling, cigarette smoking yahoos stomping through the woods making ridiculous noises.

Just so you know, none of us were allowed to carry any firearms. The only weapons we had were a knife or two.

Since the night that Bear ran from his "Mythical Creature" he hasn't talked too much about it.

Below I have attached a picture that Bear took the day after his encounter. He's lying in the same spot he was the night before, and I'm standing in the exact spot and position that the bigfoot was standing. Notice the horizontal branch about the height of my hat. Bear said that the shoulders on the bigfoot were just above the branch, and they were at least twice as wide as mine.

TIMOTHY J. O'BRIEN

I think it was back in 2015, I worked nights at a commercial HVAC call center. I got a call from a coworker who was on the roof of the building on a smoke break, He said he sees something super weird and wants me to witness it to make sure he isn't nuts. I went up to the roof ad he pointed to something at the very edge of the parking lot, a tall slender armless looing thing maybe about 7 to 8 feet tall and an off-white color. It was pacing between the trees on the far edge of the parking lot, by some houses and a road, there was a small hill that it was standing up and crouching down while appearing to look at the parking lot at the cars and employee lot.

This thing was as I said tall and armless in appearance and seemed to be very curious about looking at the lot, while at the same time not presenting itself in a manner that would show it was careless. If we were not on the roof, it would have been harder to see since it was on the far side of a slight hill between some trees. We were maybe about 800 feet away and 4 stories up, the lighting in the lot was pretty good, and there were clouds or anything in the sky. We watched the thing for about 20 minutes on several occasions it seemed to know a car was coming and crouch behind the hill. It would pace from one tree to the other and repeat that pattern for most of the time we were observing it.

After about 20 minutes we went back inside the building and were too spooked to go out again, I never did go out into the parking lot at night after that.

OZZY MASON

This encounter happened over a span of 2 days.

September 4th, 2019, at 955 pm.

It was dark and my father and I were carrying groceries into the house. We were out late and grabbed the groceries last before heading home. My dad's property is large. 19 acres that's all woods and what isn't is fenced in by barbed wire and razor wire. I was bringing the last few bags inside when I saw some eye shine under a tree branch from a large tree in the backyard. I originally dismissed it thinking it was deer or coyotes, we have a lot of them on the property, it wasn't until my dad came outside and noticed it that I took in the factors about where the eye shine was. The tree branch it was under was almost 9 and a half feet from the ground. It's the lowest branch on the tree due to us trimming it. We stayed outside and started to watch it. My dad proceeded to grab a small rock and throw it in the general area of the eyes. It didn't flinch at all and kept its eyes on us. My father and I know every animal native in East Tennessee and hunted all of them. We weren't scared of it but neither was it scared of us. Dad told me to run inside and grab my pistol, I own a Smith and Wesson M&P9 Compact M2.0 9mm pistol. I came back outside and shot 6 feet to the right of the creature. I didn't want to shoot the animal itself not knowing what it was. Cougars are native here and are illegal to kill and the possibility of it being a cougar that climbed the tree was in the back of my head. Just like when Dad threw the rock, it didn't move. After that, I told dad "Get your spotlight and shine it out there at it" He proceeded to go inside and grab it. When he came out he turned it on and as soon as it turned on the eyes vanished. He shined the light towards the branch and as he did we saw it briefly. Tall and muscular with a coat of black hair on it. Walking away upright in a bipedal stance. 3 strides and it covered a 25 ft opening between the tree and the woods. The strides happened so quickly and fluid that I couldn't get a good shot on it with my pistol. I fired 3 consecutive shots in that direction anyway. After the final shot, we heard a deep guttural yell. Almost demonic but also felt human. You felt the ground rumble as it moved and yelled. Thinking I possibly shot it blindly, I grabbed the spotlight, and my Father and I went to the area it was at. No blood or any signs of us wounding it. Just shrubs that were pressed down from it moving through. The woods my father lives in are thick and dense. It could've been 6 ft away *from us and we wouldn't have been able to see it, especially at night. We both agreed we would look around in the morning when the conditions were more suited in our favor.*

September 5th at 1030 am.

It's the following morning from our encounter last night. We loaded up our ATVs with our hunting rifles and set off to go look for it. I had my Browning X-Bolt .308 Winchester rifle along with my pistol mentioned earlier. My father brought along his Remington model 738 bolt action .270 Winchester rifle and his Sig Sauer P226 Legion. 357. We didn't want to take any chances of it possibly being a big black bear but we both knew that it wasn't. We just didn't want to accept that yet. As we came up over the large hill on the back of the property, we noticed our tripod stand was knocked over. We didn't think much about it, we had some bad storms earlier in the week and attributed it to the reason it tipped over. We then set it back up and I climbed the ladder to the top of it to get a better view around us. I noticed part of the fence was broken and laid on the ground. As if someone put so much strain on it that it snapped. The ground was flattened in the area of the broken fence. As is something moved through it numerous times. Being distracted by the fence I was paying attention to my father until he got very quiet. He spoke softly to me and told me to look at the tree about 20-25 yards in front of us. "Something large and black is behind that tree Oz," Oz being my nickname due to my middle name being Ozzy, "I can't see it all that well, but you got a better vantage point. What do you see?"

I looked and focused my vision. There are a lot of trees and finding the right one was difficult until I was looking right at it. And it was looking at me. Hiding behind the tree it would peek its head out now and then. I felt uneasy but I also didn't feel threatened. It appeared more curious than aggressive. Studying us and waiting for us to make the first move. I was hoping it forgot the fact I shot at it the night before. It had every reason to hold a grudge and charge us. Perhaps it knew we were armed? Maybe it is studying us waiting for an opening to leave or worse, attack us. I couldn't tell you. All I know is once I realized what I was looking at I informed my father about it. "Dad it's a Bigfoot. I'm not losing my shit, right?! You see it too?!" I said in the same tone he was speaking in earlier. I didn't want to spook it. I looked over at him and he nodded his head in agreement. "Son don't do anything dumb. We will lose this fight even with our firearms. Just stay calm and see what happens." After what felt like an eternity, but in reality, was probably only 5 minutes or less the

Bigfoot walked out from behind the tree and disappeared into the woods it and I both call home. I slid down the ladder and ran towards the ATVs. We parked them about 150 yards away. I jumped on it and dad followed suit and jumped on his. We left towards the house and went inside. We both were pale-faced, and my father say down and was shaking from either fear or shock. If he was feeling the same, I was then it was a combination of both. We didn't say anything for a few minutes until I said "Dab. What the hell do we do about this?" He simply said "It's bigger, faster, and more than likely smarter. Chances of it staying around here is low" we left it at that. We heard whoops the next day but after that, we never saw nor heard it again. I always go visit that area of the property when I visit my father. Just to see if it may have come back. It's been almost 3 years and I've seen zero signs. Maybe one day I'll see one again.

CAHNI KONIG

It was a large horse shaped solid figure. Too large to be a horse. There was hair flowing behind it as it moved.

I've been a paranormal investigator for a long time. As a shaman I work in the shadows. As a psychic medium I communicate with the other side. While I've had plenty of encounters with things from other realms, I've never seen or had an encounter with a Bigfoot. That is, until my team and I went to a ranch that had been having reports of different types of paranormal activity. The owners were scared and wanted answers.

It had just rained for hours but luckily it had stopped by the time we got there so we wouldn't have interference from the weather. The majority of the investigation was going to be outdoors. There were over 70 acres, and there was no way we would get to explore all of it. This was definitely not your typical house call.

I had brought quite a bit of equipment with me, and we proceeded to settle into a barn that was open on either end. We had various sensors at either end of the barn to detect movement. Some of them would light up, some of them would make noise. We had a few cat balls that we spread throughout the barn and also at either end right outside of the entrances. These small golf ball sized toys light up brightly when touched and blink. They aren't overly sensitive though, so they don't go off easily outside unless it's windy and they roll away.

I immediately connected with some strong Native American energy. It was *very clear that this had been their land. As a shaman I began to communicate with them to see if I could find out what was happening, why people at the ranch were being scared and what the natives needed. I wasn't getting all of the answers and the horses were making noises and being restless. At this time of night, all of the horses were in their stalls. I felt the need to see what was going on externally and then settle in again to communicate more.*

After exploring some of the property and coming back to the barn, I removed my body camera so I could clear out some files before turning it back on again. We were sitting in the barn when we noticed 2 cat balls going off at the rear of the barn. They weren't moving or rolling, they were stationary as they blinked. As everyone focused their attention to the activity happening at the rear of the barn something told me to look towards the front. Our vehicles were parked out that way and behind them was an open farm type split fence separating the properties. That's when I saw a massive horse shaped figure moving along the fence line. It wasn't walking the way a horse does—it was gliding, moving smoothly. It was far too large to be a horse and the way it was gliding was bizarre to say the least. It was solid and dark—I could see the hair on its mane flowing behind it as it swiftly drifted across the fence line. I stood up and pretty much yelled "WHAT IS THAT??????" It was shocking to say the least. It quickly disappeared behind a tree as my teammates came over to see what I was staring at.

My teammate, Roseanna "Red" Brookhouser and I immediately went out with flashlights to see if we could spot this creature. It was gone. There was only one tree, and then it was wide open. There was absolutely nowhere for it to go and not be seen. I was baffled. I was stunned. What I had seen was so large I know I didn't imagine it. I wasn't seeing psychically, it was physical. Energetically it didn't feel the way other things feel and I wasn't sure what to make of it. I ended up leaving with more questions than answers.

Early the next morning, Red and Kathy Westerman, (who is a seasoned Bigfoot investigator) went out to the spot along the fence line where I had seen this creature to see if there were any tracks. They found 3 sets in the grass that were still fresh from the rain the night before. A family. Two adults and one "baby". They disappeared right behind the tree where I had seen the creature go. I can't begin to express how excited I was to hear this validation! Although I wasn't able to capture my encounter on film, I was so elated to hear about the evidence they found. We will be going out there again soon. Hopefully, I will have a new part to add to my story.

ROSEANNA BROOKHOUSER

On April 30, 2022, I was called out on a paranormal investigation to help a ranch owner near Ocala, Fl, who had been having some crazy Paranormal phenomenon occurring on her ranch. She has an Airbnb on her ranch where her tenants were being terrorized by an unknown entity or entities. It got to the point where the tenants are no longer staying their entire rented stay and we're packing up and leaving in middle of the night because they couldn't take it anymore.

Kathy, a fellow teammate, and Bigfoot researcher was on location with me while we waited the rest of my team to arrive. It had been raining all evening and into the night which kept us kind of confined to the large barn where most of the activity has been found to occur. We had the barn lights on, and I went to one end of the barn to check out the storm and to take in some fresh air. I was staring into the dark rainy yard where my car was parked which was approximately 40ft away. I saw something strange standing on the driver side of my vehicle Which would place it between the dumpster and my car. It was a good 3 1/2-4 feet taller than my car which is a 2013, Lincoln MKS sedan, and I just saw a black outline & what looked to be goldish amber eyes and black/grey wet, shiny cheeks and that's all I could make out of what I thought was a face. I didn't freak out I just kind of stared in disbelief of what I was looking yet and thought my eyes are playing tricks on me because of the rain. It was just staring at me. I kept my eyes on it while I called Kathy over to see what I was looking at, but as she came over and asked me what was wrong, I glanced at her for a quarter of a second glance back pointing at my car and said what's that and as it came on my mouth, I realized it was no longer standing there. Kathy thought I was kind of crazy and said it was just a reflection of the dumpster, but I saw the dumpster too and that's not what I saw. This happened shortly before midnight.

Approximately 2 1/2 hours later the rest of my team finally had arrived shortly after that first incident, and we continued our investigation. Cahni and Barbara are both psychic mediums and shamans, and they both are putting themselves into a meditative state which is similar to self-hypnosis they call "going on a journey." I myself am a Reiki practitioner and was also meditating and concentrating on the energy around me and about 10-15 minutes into it, our paranormal balls sitting outside the back door started strobing red and blue lights which I could see through my eyelids, so I open my eyes and realize that the balls have been triggered. Cat balls, aka paranormal balls are only triggered by touch and we use it for Ghost Hunting and allow for spirits to communicate to us through them to let us know that they're with us. As I got the teams attention to let them know what was going on we started walking towards the Paranormal balls taking pictures and video and at that very moment something had cut Cahni's attention at the opposite end of the barn outside just a little bit further past from where my car was parked earlier, and she started screaming, "What is that?!! What the fuck is that!???" Cahni and I started running towards what she had seen, and she described it as a large, tall mass gliding across the yard which part of it towered two or 3 feet above the back of the truck that it was passing behind. And she said it didn't look like it had a walking motion like it was bobbing up and down or anything, just a smooth glide. I shine my military flashlight towards where it would be, but we couldn't see anything we could just hear lots of slashing through the wet grass. Even though I didn't see what she claimed she saw, I completely believed her. I had never seen her react that way and all the years I've known her, it was genuine confusion and fear. I told her I think you just saw your first Sasquatch. Up until that point I hadn't told her what I saw just a couple hours earlier before she got there. Cahni wasn't much of a believer of Bigfoot until then. The next morning about 7:30 I grabbed a cup of coffee and went out to where the entities were seen and found over 24 footprints in three different sizes in the fresh wet grass ranging from 16 inches, 13 inches, and 7 inches. (This is an area of the ranch where nobody walks nor are there any children on the property ever.) The owner of the ranch and I cast the 16-inch print.

Five years earlier the owner casted the exact same size and shape print in her neighbor's woods behind her house. Five of the surrounding ranches have all claimed to have seen or encountered Bigfoot on their property. We believe that this particular night we had the entire family walk through the ranch yard. My personal theory is that the paranormal balls going off we're just a distraction so they could pass by. this is an ongoing investigation, and we have two more scheduled trips coming up before the end of July to see what else we can uncover.

The next encounter was a phone interview, and I transcribed it; I hope it comes out as well as it was told to me. Justin England has a great encounter and a great podcast; check him out on *Cryptids of the Corn* podcast.

JUSTIN ENGLAND

Over a two-year period, 2011–2012, Justin and his family had odd things happening around their farm. Their farm bumped up to a large patch of wood, which separated them from three other families. In May of 2011, things like finding the large grain bin top open. At first the family blamed each other for leaving it open, and other things around the farm had been moved with no explanation.

On July 4, Justin finished his closing shift at McDonald's and drove home, his family had gone to the lake, but it was late, around 11 p.m., so he decided to go home and meet them the next day. He was kicked back on the couch, eating a snack and watching TV, but the dogs were acting crazy. All three dogs, including the big Lab, were whining and trying to get on his lap. Then he heard three big bangs, didn't think much about it; after all, it was the Fourth of July. Then the three bangs seem to be getting closer; after about the third or fourth time, he wondered if it was his friend Nick. He called up Nick and asked his if he was doing it, but Nick told him they were in Pennsylvania.

There is a huge dead tree beside the barn not far from the house. Then Justin heard three loud bangs on the dead tree; with the way the dogs were acting, Justin was terrified. Then three more bangs came from the side of the barn, scaring the horses, causing then to run out of the barn into the field. Justin realized he'd better not move because the front wall, which is all glass, was the only thing between him and whoever was banging. Then, not but a few feet from the house was his brother's beater car, and three very loud booms came from the car. Justin was beyond terrified. Suddenly he heard his uncle coming down their driveway with music blaring.

The next day his dad and a friend of his dad who was ex-law enforcement were looking around where Justin had heard the banging. The ex-cop and his dad saw four big dents in the side of the barn and decided someone had hit it with a sledgehammer, because of the height and depth of the dents.

When things continued to happen, it was blamed on the guy, but everything stopped in August. Nothing odd happened on the farm through fall or winter, but in May it started again, but this time it was more disrupting. Things are *being piled up high; the grain bin left open. But the last straw was when their expensive chickens started disappearing. Chickens worth up to $800 disappearing from a very secure coop. Something with intelligence had to turn a latch to get to the chickens.*

So his dad bought a red heeler dog to protect the farm. The dog was trained to protect the farm animals from wildlife. Then one night the dog was raising cain, and Justin and his brother decide to walk down to where the dog was and knock out whatever the dog had treed. They walked down with a baseball bat and a golf club, but the dog was having a fit at the four-wheeler trail, and there were no trees there. They walked up to the dog, and that was when they saw it. Two very large yellowish eyes looking at them, eight feet in the air; the eyes would slowly blink. They were filled with fear, but they knew not to run. Justin and his brother slowly backed up, but after about ten feet, the fear was more than they could handle, and they broke and ran to the house.

They told their dad. He said he'd had enough of this guy and grabbed his shotgun and headed to where the dog was. He stopped by the dog and yelled out, "Whoever you are, step out, or I will fire." He started counting down from ten, and no one stepped out, so he took aim at the top of the trees and fired. When the shotgun fired, it sounded like a herd of buffalo bursting from the woods just ten feet from him, headed deeper into the woods. Their dad came back into the house, where he told his wife and older kids that it was not a man and not to talk about it. After that, no more Bigfoot activity.

Justin, my friend, I hope I did your story justice.

CONCLUSION

I wrote this book to introduce creatures of this world that the mainstream refuses to acknowledge. I want my readers to open their minds to the unusual things that do exist all over the world. Thank you for reading, and I hope you enjoyed this reference guide to the monsters that creep in the night.

If you enjoyed this book check out George Lunsford's book:
Legends, Myths, Monsters, and Ghosts

ABOUT THE AUTHOR

George Lunsford has done many jobs from being a maintenance man to making explosives for the government. He was also an actor for many years doing indie feature films, commercials, book trailers, public service videos, and even a music video for the Steep Canyon Rangers called Long Shot.

George's life was changed when he was a young man. His great-grandmother passed away and her spirit visited him one night, sitting on the foot of his bed. She looked at him and said I love you, said goodbye and disappeared. He wanted to believe it was just a dream but could smell her scent in his room.

George attended a haunted high School. In his early twenties he had a near death experience from pneumonia. He saw his own body in the bed and a lady that had died in that hospital room stood there talking to him. He saw the Angel of death as he opened a portal of bright light. The spirit that was talking to him, told him "It's not your time". He laid back down and woke up to alarms going off and nurses busting into hospital room.

George also had encounters in the Bermuda Triangle, a UFO in the middle of the ocean, and many other events. George has always been interested in paranormal, cyprid creatures, and Bigfoot and has done a lot of research thought his lifetime.

George wrote "Legends, Myth, Monsters, and Ghost" series because he wanted to share the stories he's heard and researched from all over the US with the world. He wants people to know that there is so much out in the world, then in that little bubble we all live in. When we were young, the older people would pass these stories down and we would go out and try to see if they were real. He hopes that sharing these stories, will give everyone an adventure to go on. George being an old sailor has had many adventures both at sea and on land. Please enjoy his books and go on your own adventure. Be safe!!!!

You can contact the author through his website: authorgeorgelunsford.x1ohost.com

You may share your thoughts on his book, theory, and podcast. You can get links from his website.

instagram.com/georgelunsford329

ALSO BY GEORGE LUNSFORD

Legends Myths Monsters and Ghosts

www.ingramcontent.com/pod-product-compliance
Lightning Source LLC
Chambersburg PA
CBHW022329280326
41934CB00006B/584